"NOT FALLING IN LOVE AT FIRST SIGHT IS PERHAPS THE COMMONEST EXPERIENCE OF THE MODERN WORLD."

With clearly infallible reasoning (note the quote above), Stephen Potter lays down the rules of Anti-Woo. His latest book is an outspoken manual on the joys and securities of non-love and an uproarious delight to the avid cultists of Pottermanship.

In a series of case histories Potter describes every kind of entraping female from Clinging Vine to Competent Careerist, the plain ones and the beautiful. Beauty, Potter admits, poses a special problem in Anti-woomanship, but he shows that it is not an insurmountable one.

Potter's advice to the practitioners of Anti-Woo (the men) can best be summed up by one of his Basic Techniques headed: The Importance of Being Noble . . . and its subdivision: If You Can't Be Noble, Attack.

"THE DEFINITIVE WORK"—San Rafael
Independent Journal

STEPHEN POTTER, who graduated from Merton, Oxford, describes his career as a failed academic lecturer, failed literary biographer, failed editor, failed dramatic critic, failed book critic and failed rowing blue. To restore the situation he then invented GAMESMANSHIP, LIFEMANSHIP, and ONE-UPMANSHIP codified techniques of subtly ignoble beh̶ claims he no longer prac̶ cticed against him.

William M. Gaines's
MAD Humor from SIGNET
(50¢ each)

To Our Readers: If your dealer does not have the SIGNET and MENTOR books you want, you may order them by mail enclosing the list price plus 10¢ a copy to cover mailing. (New York City residents add 5% Sales Tax. Other New York State residents add 2% only plus any local sales or use taxes.) If you would like our free catalog, please request it by postcard. The New American Library, Inc., P. O. Box 2310, Grand Central Station, New York, N. Y. 10017.

THE FIRST LIFEMANSHIP GUIDE

ANTI-WOO

by Stephen Potter

THE LIFEMAN'S IMPROVED PRIMER FOR NON-
LOVERS. WITH SPECIAL CHAPTERS ON WHO
NOT TO LOVE, FALLING OUT OF LOVE, AVOID-
ANCE GAMBITS, AND COAD-SANDERSON'S SCALE
OF PROGRESSIVE RIFTS.

These essays are sponsored by the Lifemanship
Trust, Yeovil, in association with Comex Chem-
icals, 95-97 Hyde Road, Braintree, (Eng.)

Illustrated by Lt-Col. Frank Wilson

A SIGNET BOOK

Published by THE NEW AMERICAN LIBRARY

Published as a SIGNET BOOK
by arrangement with McGraw-Hill Book Company,
who have authorized this softcover edition.
A hardcover edition is available from
McGraw-Hill Book Company.

FIRST PRINTING, SEPTEMBER, 1966

SIGNET TRADEMARK REG. U.S. PAT. OFF. AND FOREIGN COUNTRIES
REGISTERED TRADEMARK—MARCA REGISTRADA
HECHO EN CHICAGO, U.S.A.

SIGNET BOOKS are published by
The New American Library, Inc.
1301 Avenue of the Americas, New York, New York 10019

PRINTED IN THE UNITED STATES OF AMERICA

To H. J.
who
By what she is and what she does
Makes nonsense of the undoubted wisdom
of these pages

Contents

CONTENTS

1

Introductory

I want to say something of the genesis of this book, and of the new series of *Lifemanship Guides* on which we are working. But first let us set down, in order to clarify ourselves as much as anyone else, the key dates marking the establishment of Lifemanship in world thought. It will be of some interest to notice the slowness of the early growth, followed by another period of slowness.

> *Summer (?) 1924.* First trauma. Slightly older and better dressed man at picnic turns inattentively to the youthful Potter and says:
> 'Let's see, you play the piano or something?'
> 'Yes, sort of,' says Potter, unable to think of anything else.

1927. The 'Village Cricket Letter'. Meynell writes to Potter to ask him what tactics Great Yeldham should employ against Sudbury.

'Try Gamesmanship' writes Potter, using word for first time and attempting first crude definition:— 'something between the sporting and the unsporting.'

1927–33. 'The Sunshine Interval'. A small group of friendly, or fairly friendly, men treat Gamesmanship as friendly by-play, a joke, or 'kidding'.

1932. Potter's first-hand observation of Joad's lawn tennis gambit:—the early use, against young and gentlemanly opponents, of the phrase 'kindly say clearly please whether the ball is in or out'. Realization of the possible agentative value of Gamesmanship.

1932–46. The Assimilative Years.

1947 February. Record hard winter. Fuel cut. National crisis. Potter writes first draft of Gamesmanship.

'The First Draft'. Original painting by A. V. de Sozo A.R.A. now in the collection of Mrs Frida Wert.

May. Famous London publisher is lukewarm.

June. Potter, then little known as writer, meets then little known publisher, Hart-Davis. Together they co-opt then little-known Colonel, Wilson, as statistical clarifier and diagramatic craftsman (often called 'illustrator').

August. Meanwhile, in background, Denis Compton achieves highest number of centuries in a season.

November. Publication of Gamesmanship. Founder thinks of answer to Question put in 1924 ('you play the piano or something?') * Forms the word 'Lifemanship', and self-evolves the first lifemanship gambit.

1948. Gamesmanship accepted in coastal states of North America.

1949–56. Period of open publication. Period of world acceptance. Stevenson Democratic candidate.

1956. Idea of Lifemanship Guides formulated and shelved.

1956–64. Period of gestation.

1964. First Lifemanship Guide.

1965. Attention focused on hitherto little-known publisher, McGraw-Hill by their sponsorship of the first Lifemanship Guide.

Genesis of the Guides

Most of the original *Lifemanship* consisted of short chapters on subjects often not closely related. Is there a genuine

---

* In its earliest form, this answer was 'Yes I do, but *(more firmly)* not the sort of piano-playing you would be interested in, I'm afraid.'

relationship between Week-endmanship and the Canterbury Block? But it is wrong to say that these chapters were put in for padding. Any suggestion that the themes are obvious, however, I applaud. They are *so obvious that nobody has ever thought of writing about them before*. In fact that is the essence of the Lifemanship Guides. What a wealth of psycho-philosophical comment could be added here, were it not that our aim is brevity!

The Norfolk style.

We are always proud of the fact that it was a young Yeovil Extension student who thought it worth while to set down the first guide to safety-razor shaving.*

Soon we realized that other subjects, just as important as shaving, had been equally neglected. Here was new grist to our mill and the little coke stove in the research room at Correspondence College smoked away more merrily than it had done for years. 'At the Wheel' has fallen behind

* Albert Grassman's 210 page pamphlet included his now well-known comparative diagrams of shaving gestures taken county by county. Here are the first measurings of 'bugle-blowers cheek' as a skin tautener and its counterpart 'hangman's neck', (the upstretched chin). These results were graphed with income groups and graded with black- and unblack-coated workers. Grassman was no mere statistician but took an interest in the human side as well. For those who went out of doors in broad sunlight, he recommended the removal of the tiny smoke-stained tuft of lip hair just below the nose. He had a kind of humour, too. For upper class hosts greeting female dinner guests, he recommended 'a good scrape at 7 p.m., on the side of the right chin'.

schedule owing, we all feel, to lack of co-operation from the Minister of Transport: but a certainty for 1966, with all of us contributing, is *How to be One Up on the Young,* with its sister dialogues devoted to How to make the Old feel Older.

Curiously, this present work, which we approached as 'How Not to Be in Love without Actual Thwarting', though far more difficult, was first off the production line. In a way it was the extreme delicacy of the problems which egged us on. Typically, Odoreida thought this would be a splendid opportunity for what he called being absolutely fearless. But Odoreida being fearless about sex turned out on inspection to be a series of sentences in *the majority* of which he brought in one of the five words not usually printed.

'What's this?' we said.

'One has to be absolutely fearless,' he said.

'Fearless of what danger?' we said.

'I mean you can use asterisks,' Odoreida went on, wheezily. 'Top writers——'

'Yes, but asterisks are only fairly fearless.' Cogg Willoughby took him up sharply.

'You've only got to count them,' Odoreida said, wheezing up for a long cough.

I can only say that when Odoreida handed in his contribution he was keeping up the asterisks right to the last sentence of the last page, which was actually headed **** ****.

Let us forget Odoreida and say right out that this book, like other Yeovil works, is for family reading, though some people have said that the family we have in mind is a peculiar one.*

---

* Following Lifemanship's never failing technique of keeping ahead in trends or fashions by taking one step backwards, we are inaugurating a new self-censorship, decidedly more rigid than any in force since the War. This involves a new Back to Bowdler movement, though we now feel that Bowdler did not go far enough. We are actually bringing out new editions of the classics in which, without altering the general sense, new words are substituted for any which may have unpleasant connotations. Here are a few examples, with our corrections in italics:

Above the acres of the rye   She *adopted* so many children
  Damp with faint praise   she didn't know what to do
Hull hath no fury like a woman scorned

The subject of not being in love is so well known and so much a part of almost everybody's life that until we made the break-through it was becoming impossible to mention it. By some sort of unspoken international agreement, although plays and poems and anthologies about falling in love appear every day, falling out of love, by contrast, is given an extraordinarily poor showing. In the same way, we are brought up to believe that 'all the world loves a lover': yet the truth is that people in love are unreliable, incapable of relaxing, anxious to give embarrassing proofs that their characters have changed for the better, and incapable of concentrating for more than twenty seconds (the record is said to be 36 seconds). Moreover, because things are always going either *(a)* tremendously well with them or *(b)* appallingly badly, they must tell somebody about it immediately or burst.

Coad-Sanderson taking no notice of slightly pornographic poster.

By contrast, the happiness of not being in love is like coming out of a rush-hour Underground in a hot August and stepping straight into the loneliness of leafy country, with a couple of old retired horses vaguely munching in the distance.

How, then, to avoid the supposedly unavoidable? And if unavoidable how to back out bloodlessly? An exhausting handicap of being in love is the absence of dead water. One of the pair is always a little more so than the other, and this includes vice versa. Hence the difficulties of graceful detachment. The first gentle step backwards is a starting gun for an all-out chase by the other party.

These problems are universal, yet hitherto there has been no Encyclopaedia to present everything historically, no Bædeker to triple star most favoured methods, no Guide Michelin to rehabilitation centres, no de Brett to regulate the hierarchy of leading non-lovers, no Wisden to codify the details and give lists of record scores. We are said to have fought for the Four Freedoms: but in the shelves of our public libraries there is no space for the fifth, freedom from loving.

It may be remembered that a few notes on the counterpart of Anti-woo—Woomanship—appeared in a chapter in *Lifemanship*. We have always prided ourselves on the positive approach. We have gone further. We have admitted that except in special circumstances love is greater than lifemanship. It is in the transmigration of the individual to the fields of non-love, and the cautious avoidance of love as a general rule, that the techniques of lifemanship will be found we believe, indispensable.

Lesser-known incident in Pyramus and Thisbe saga. After conversing for 9 years, Pyramus attempts to close gap in wall.

2

The Climate of Anti-Woo

We have nowhere said that men and women should never marry. We believe that in certain circumstances such unions should exist between consenting adults.

But the often repeated dictum that 'there is one woman in the world for you, (cf. 'Wait for Mr Right') implies unequivocally that there are approximately 2,105,600,000 women who are, or will when they are old enough, be wrong.

In order to recognize Right, then, it is necessary to make group reconnaissances of situations in which Woo is contra-indicated.* Not falling in love at first sight is perhaps the commonest experience of the modern world: yet the student of anti-woo should learn to recognize quickly signs, situations and latent inter-personality sequences wherein the future possibility of woo must be comprehended and avoided.

First Lessons for Men

Any man who accepts an invitation to a mixed party is in some degree associating himself with the possibility of an

* This book has been read by pretty well scores of specialists. I have asked for their independent comments and criticisms. I have added the initials of the critic when these are worth printing and when I can answer wittily back. Here for instance 'C-W' writes ' "contra-indicated". Why do you copy the habit of dragging in half understood medical terms?' 'Half-understood by whom?' I replied at once.

attack on the independence of his woo isolation. He should learn to recognize undesirables instantly. Take the outwardly rather crushed looking girl to whom he offers a cigarette. Now if instead of refusing it with a scarcely perceptible gesture, she speaks, then let this be a first microscopic warning.

'No thanks, I don't smoke.' Perhaps her intonation will be bright and clear, falsely suggesting that this is a good opening for a conversation.

'Thanks I don't smoke'. Worse still, there may be a hint of slightly refined reproach. Observe now the handsome chrysanthemum expert who starts by saying something about her daughter.

'I haven't the faintest idea whether Julie is here or not. What can you do with them?'

This means that she is going to talk exclusively of her children. How refreshingly quiet, by contrast, is Mrs Tasker, who has just asked for a gin and tonic with very little gin. Her slow voice and long wondering pauses are attractive, but does not her skin look a shade too soft to be credible? Has it not just gone over the border? Is it not probable that she was drinking her first gin and tonic when she got up, at 10:30?

Probably no need to warn against Miss G., who, perhaps because she is tremendously quietly dressed, has the look of someone who is going to say something unfair about somebody in less than three minutes. Watch how she stares at the level of the eighth thoracic vertebra of Georgie, the girl standing with her back to us. Yet Georgie will be no temptation, if only because her vacant, open-air eye suggests that she resents the time she is wasting here, away from her favourite pony. Winkle, her sister, is not quite with you either. Her unenthusiastic look, when she talks to you, suggests that the man in her mind's eye is either a wonderfully sophisticated middle-aged Rally driver of twenty-six, or the remarkably unburnished looking double-bass who plays pizzicato in the Root and Rhythm Five.

Only one amongst us, one whose name I will for the time being withhold, will be tempted to parley with Winkle.

Critical approach towards other women's clothes ploy.
Angle of glance towards eighth thoracic vertebra.

But another sort of danger approaches. Look at the easy freedom with which those two loveless men are talking.

'I think we might pop off soon', one says, happy, inconsequent. They talk with the perfect spontaneity of the unattached. But whose voice is this?

'Now then James, Duncan, I can't have you two talking together all the time. There are some beautiful ladies I want you to meet'.

This is the hostess, and at once we are in the realm of Lifemanship. More probably she has said 'For heaven's sake don't just get bogged down—*help* me.' But whatever her wording, hostess is able, by careful inflection, to imply that the group of three women to whom she refers just have not got the attraction for men which, as one example, she has. By thus forcing the males and the females to speak to each other, hostess is *herself creating an anti-woo situation*, perhaps because at some level of consciousness,* she has herself in mind as the ultimate woo object.

But suppose the segregated women are in fact unattractive. Suppose one is dressed in a sort of hot black velvet with a trace of dust round the shoulders, reminding you of being forced to stay in your great aunt's dining room when you were longing to play in the garden. You can see something is wrong before you speak to her. 'I want you to meet Phoebe Middlewick', says the hostess, and accentuates the name in a way which sinks the girl before introduction. From a distance, too, it is obvious that this girl wishes to emphasize, by her clothes, her tweedy resistance to a party. Alternatively she may be too irritatingly twinkling, too pinned about by small ornaments, including a clasp representing a small radar aerial. Or if her shoulders are partially bare, they may yet reveal one piece of rigging too many. Or maybe she entered the room too quickly and busily, plop-plop-plopping on the parquet. Or it is just some physical thing about the legs—her feet, ankles, calves seem to be assembled from three different jigsaw puzzles;

* 'level of consciousness' is absurd. It is misleading to give the faculty of knowing a three dimensional stratification, like a club sandwich C-S. S.P.: Nonsense. All phrases with 'levels' in them, particularly 'at different levels', are top o.k. for 1963–5.

or she may have a pair of peculiarly hairy, or even woolly eyebrows which nearly meet in the middle, and affect one at a distance with an unpleasant tickling sensation on the mucous membranes of the palate.

Anti-love lifemanship should come to the aid of a man stuck with one of these. It is vulgar technique to employ tricks of an outmoded and obvious kind.

Do not say 'Let me get you a drink', and then slink off and keep out of her sight: don't say 'Look—my wife wants to meet you. May I get her?' The essential thing is to leave the girl complimented but too puzzled to reply, so that you can pretend to take her silence as a delicate dismissal. E.g.

1. Start with a swingeing compliment: ('I think Mr Dior has been using your face—hasn't he? In the glossies? To heighten the effect of mink?') Then look as if you feel you may have gone too far, and disappear.

2. Similarly, begin 'You won't remember me. Stage 4, Pinewood, '62.'

Only one girl in 5,000 will say she has never had anything to do with films in her life. You can then get away instantly if you add, in a lower voice, 'See you at the Three farthings tonight, I shouldn't be surprised?'

3. Briefer exit lines need a certain virtuosity. But if the tone of voice is approximately correct a simple 'I wanted just to say "hallo", if only for five seconds, before I left' is a good quick one.

4. Or 'Alas, I have someone "in tow". Let's speak later.'

5. If girl is not susceptible to semi-romantic appoach, try the humdrum 'Good God. We mustn't be the last to leave. I have got to get her out of this' (wave to the opposite corner of the room as if to escortee) 'Wish we could have talked'.

6. Try, as a long shot, 'Well, I like *people*. Don't you? Thought you did' (step backwards, looking intently at the roots of the girl's hair, like in the films).

7. I myself have been making increasing use lately of 'Excuse me, I'm not supposed to stand'. For this purpose, I need, and have, a stick. It is important that the girl should not attempt to follow you to the chair towards which you pretend to be manoeuvring.

Eighth method of painlessly leaving woman within twelve seconds of introduction.

'Anything wrong?' Gattling typically said.

'My talisman', I had to reply, with a meaningless wink. But many are now using these sticks.

8. Although this final ploy can only be used once, I still prefer, however: 'You wrote me a very beautiful letter after my late loss. I shall always treasure it.' Don't look directly at the girl when you say this. Immediately afterwards, walk diagonally away.

Significance of Beauty in the Male/Female plexus

A year ago Western TV videotaped a discussion, organized by myself, and including two of our Yeovil staff. This has not yet been publicly shown. It may be that some of the conclusions are too subversive for family viewing, for we had a doctor on the panel. We have our own Yeovil School of Medical Behaviouristics, and are hoping to convert the B.M.A. to our belief that no general physician or surgeon should practise without being a fully qualified psychiatrist as well.

During the discussion the Doctor, who was anonymous even to us, said, in reply to a question:

DOCTOR: Men who come within *the ambience* of a woman, are more likely to be attracted by, *to feel the attraction of,* that woman, if she is beautiful.

I must have forgotten the circumstances, my surroundings, everything when I said

POTTER: You mean they are more likely to fall in love with them if they are pretty?
DOCTOR: Yes.

We were extremely glad to get this statement from 'Nonny', as we called our anonymous consultant.*

This proves that good looks are the natural enemy of Anti-Woo, and that the first hurdle is the most difficult. Beauty is the classical One-Up state, and the true Lifeman must be determined to try to counter this, however unfavourable the circumstances. Let us take the woman known as Warlingham first, because she was the 'perfect' beauty. The features were so exactly right, the skin so smooth and textureless, that the whole effect was not of shape or pro-

---

* When we had drinks after the recording, 'Nonny' threw aside the last shred of his reserves and freely volunteered that 'most—about 88%—of men are *less* likely to be attracted if the woman is *not* pretty.' He was not of course, using scientific terms.

portion but one of total pang. In the language of inappropriate poetical comparison her 'eyes are like stars.' Actually we advise you, to help you as a start, to look at those large wet glistening objects more carefully and realize that they are much more like jelly-fish than stars.

But whatever happens, you will look. No expert should have difficulty in staring without seeming to be rude. He does not say 'haven't we met before', or 'you remind me', but *'Five* years is the limit of any one parliament, isn't it' or 'I've just remembered I ought to have caught the 3.10 for Pulborough', or 'You wouldn't—couldn't—remember the comedian, Danny Kaye? . . .' Listen, and watch, to see if there is any reaction whatever. Drop your eyes to the swan-like neck, except of course that the curve is not like a swan, but (if you turn to our list of alternative similes) the replica of the southern entry to the Doncaster bypass. In some men, absolute lack of response sparks off a determination to make some impression: and it was on just such occasions as this that, thirty-nine years ago, for the first time, I self-recognized the existence of lifemanship and evolved a self gambit to overcome loss of face.*

What does the man do against No Response? How does he deal with that wonderful complexion, so smooth and textureless that all curves and shadows merge; that skin like marble (corrected simile: like peeled pear)?

Layman may say to himself 'I am not attracted to this girl. Obviously she is simply mad about her own looks. Probably narcy. Since there is no trace of lines on her skin, even about her mouth, she cannot possibly have a grain of humour. She wants teaching a lesson. I am the one to do it.'

Needless to say, this approach is the usual first step to total slavery. At the very moment when Layman will feel that he is getting his own way, it will be the girl, Warlingham, who gives the order, more piercingly exact, though unspoken, than a drill sergeant. Taken out in the evening, she does not actually refuse, on a dry night, to walk eight yards along the pavement towards the restaurant door, or

* These terms were not of course then in use. This event took place at a house near Platts Fields, Manchester.

the theatre entrance, because that would force you, the escort, to drive, after you have dropped her at the very toes of a commissionaire, towards a one-way block facing the wrong direction. She does not refuse, but you will find yourself in that block nevertheless, facing the wrong direction: and when you come back she will certainly be talking to a friend she has found, a man without style, shorter and tubbier than yourself, wearing an unsuitable black-striped shirt, and making the girl laugh like a cockatoo.

Female Beauty and the Lifeman

How, then, does the lifeman deal with female beauty? 'Yeovil has failed us here', it is occasionally said: and this is partly true. There is no doubt that older methods of being somewhat caddish and not caring a damn sometimes work; so does a reputation for knowing beautiful women. We ourselves trained six of these, who lived locally, to come up and kiss us affectionately, or rather with affectionate camaraderie, whenever they saw us with a girl. Or even, wearing pretty hats, just to wave, over people's heads. But the fees involved were heavy and we were the victim of the laziness and dissatisfaction of the workers.

Another line of approach is to contrive some method of making the point that there is only one year in a woman's life—perhaps only one month or even week—when beauty is at its peak. A few days later it is then always possible to say 'why I didn't recognize her' in such a way as to suggest that the girl has already gone two yards over the hill.

A difficult case is the beautiful girl who is still more remarkable because she is French or perhaps Indian or Malaysian, and can therefore enhance the imperious quality of her beauty by a kind of *foreign immobility*.* She has no language problem because she rarely speaks, except

* 'Keeps them on their toes', said Zahlia Denesti, whose real name, I happened to know, was Shirley Biggs.

to rattle off her native language in an undertone, to some frighteningly possessed and equally foreign escort. In conversation with Briton, be he layman or lifeman, she will suggest that English men as a class are childishly games loving, football watchers, grouse shooters, Club or pub men, and therefore clumsy in their attentions to women. 'Oh for the kind of treatment I get in Courbuse', they seem to suggest, as if they were used to the distillation of millenniums of polished elegance from their non-English escorts. Even a reasonably sophisticated Englishman feels himself turning into a sort of Mr Kipps in her presence, showing long pink wrists.

STUDENT: Can the lifeman counter?

EXPERT: He can tell this particular foreign woman, Talloires, that she ought to visit the British Museum.

STUDENT: Why?

EXPERT: She will feel uneasy for a moment. Alternatively he can ask her the way to the British Museum.

STUDENT: How do you mean?

EXPERT: It is sometimes possible to build up a counter-impression of an internationalism so complete that the position of such a landmark even of your own country is mixed up in your mind with say, the whereabouts of the Musea Antiqua in Santiago. True internationalism is one-up on any degree of the merely foreign.

STUDENT: Anything else?

EXPERT: Very little. Make rapid asides to some fellow-lifeman in an accent which suggests that you are speaking Egyptian for security reasons.

Mention of the perfect profile of Warlingham reminds us of a closely related type also requiring counter-measures. This is Beaulieu, an Ex-perfect Profile. She may be an actress whom now younger people do not perfectly remember—perhaps because, boringly, they had not been born—though the fact that she was the second best in *Private Lives* after Gertrude Lawrence, or was chosen for the truly great part of the nun in the last truly great story

made into a truly great film by Gustaversen, gives her a romantic interest which has a certain woo potential.

Watch her, now, going through the drill of being a beauty. The young man talking to her is made nervous by the smell of scent, and fumbles, when she searches for her handbag, with his squashed packet of cork tipped, two of which have exploded. Five hundred to one she will say 'I always smoke these' and pick one from the tiny gold case as exactly as if it were an asparagus tip out of season. Fumbling with a book match, man will at any rate show he is trying, and he can have another good sniff at that good scent: but he will want to get away.

Personally I like Beaulieu. She is quite a warm hearted old megalith. I like talking about theatrical yesterdays as if they were todays. And I am quite prepared to agree pro or con any young dramatist she likes. In fact the danger is that as she gets older one may like her too much. There is a certain pleasing vagueness nowadays—one galosh left on, at the party, an eyebrow not yet pencilled in. Occasionally she will cut a dramatic critic on principle, most likely one too young to have ever even heard her name. But if you have a weakness for Beaulieu do remember that she is inclined to reveal a foot or two of splendid shoulder at unsuitable moments, often associated with some jewel apparently glued on to the skin surface. Huge aquamarines at a polo match may lead to women staring sideways at Beaulieu with covert concentration as if they were looking at a street accident. Watch for this.

Non woo-worthiness of Non-doers

Women who have no job now represent only twelve per cent of the population, according to L.G.O.*

Yet more than one warning is needed here. To start with, there is the occupation of having no occupation, because there is nobody, at present, who doesn't do anything.

* Lifemanship Guess Organization.

RESEARCH PERSON: What does *she* do?

FRIEND: How do you mean?

RESEARCH PERSON: What does she *do?*

FRIEND: Well, she's really an organizer—she has a gift for it—she came in on the charity dance at the Winchester—she worked in the canteen—she had a term at the Brompton place—she said two lines in the Battle of the Nile film—she can type well without actually doing shorthand (she says she can write longhand almost as quickly)—she's learning Russian——.

In other words, when she is married she will have no occupation of any kind whatever. My friend Morton Overdrive always had a soft spot for this kind of woman. He himself came from a vaguely humble family.

' "In my mother's day," she tells me,' he said, adding an exclamation mark, 'You never asked people "what they did".'

Overdrive's first brush with a non-doer came when he met Sandgate. She believed that woman could attract by quick powers of comprehension. Nobody could have been easier to comprehend quickly than Overdrive: but Sandgate became so intuitive, she anticipated his mood so sensitively, that she practically ran the whole mood herself.

SANDGATE: This weekend, you'll want to get right outside yourself.

OVERDRIVE: Will I?

SANDGATE: Mentally, you've been sitting in the same position too long.

The fact was that Overdrive began drinking sherry at 12:00, and it soon made him feel sleepy. When he did really get down to checking his accounts and fiddling about with papers, Sandgate would 'see he was busy', and make tiptoe appearances in order not to disturb him, which disturbed him. Sandgate was kind and women liked her: but she watched your face when she first saw you.

SANDGATE: You know you're not really *ordinary* this morning.

OVERDRIVE: I am really ordinary.

SANDGATE (*disbelieving*): Are you really an ordinary boy?

When she said this Overdrive would take his one-eyed golden labrador Susan for a walk across the fields. This shows how strongly he felt because walks in the country with this dog Susan were hell.

On the rebound, Overdrive linked up with no-work girl No. 2, the warm-hearted semi-Bavarian Hilde—strong, uninhibited, no touch of psycho, warm, fond of children. But our Anti-woo Aid Society slid into action (Overdrive was a registered Lifeman) and were able to reconstruct his future with its Trait Evolution Computer, correct to a 25% error.

'If Hilde and Overdrive were to marry' said the machine, in computerese 'this light, spontaneous girl, shy and obedient, would grow in girth. Before long she would be taking up a lot of space, physically. And as for psychological lebensraum, in two months she would need a small suite all to herself.'

Overdrive liked to do some of his actuarial work at home.

He had built himself a sort of lock-up as a refuge: but concentration on his own life was not truly possible. Hilde could pass through doors, as if they were made of stage steam from the last Act of *Don Giovanni*. The cooking of two chops, the bronchial bouts of a cousin one hundred miles distant, or the fact that the water was taking a long time to drain out of her bath—such incidents engulfed the house and flooded through the working day. If Hilde were only six weeks pregnant, no household, business or artistic activity could even be mentioned. In her hands, anything remotely decent about the historically o.k. position of infants in the household became a bore and a penance to everybody else.

> STUDENT: *But surely if you're producing a child* . . .
> COMPUTER: Quite. But.
> STUDENT: You mean that in some way—
> COMPUTER: There would, if she had a job, be stimulus-shared-expression-opposite-interests.
> STUDENT (*pressing different knob*): What . . . I mean who . . .
> COMPUTER (*tripped by this ambiguity*): Soda and bicycles.

Dangers of Bouncing

The point about Hilde is that long before there was a sign of any family, she would reveal herself as one of those women who immediately after marriage produce from nowhere a constantly multiplying band of camp followers, advocates, supporters, yes-women, cousins, old school friends, and pious nondescripts all inclined to support her with an 'Oh you poor dear' expression.

Poor old Overdrive. He saw our point, particularly after he had met some of the English relatives of Hilde. But (poor old* Overdrive) he was the bugbear of anti-wooman-

* 'poor old'. In the *Concise Lifemanship Dictionary*, the first meaning of 'poor old' is 'ha-ha, not like me'.

ship because he was an inveterate bouncer. In other words if he got out of one woo situation, he was so exhilarated that he immediately rebounded into another one, diagonally opposite. Overdrive was a sloppy dresser. He seemed unhappy unless one shirt button was undone: sometimes they would all unbutton together, spontaneously. He left his shoelaces untied till about 11 a.m. This was before he rebounded in the direction of Clare, a friendship which was to lead to those screaming fits of Overdrive. Now, by using our simple medicaments, he only utters an occasional smiling moan, though he still smells faint expensive scent when there isn't any.

Clare was certainly the opposite of Hilde. Daughter of an obscure Suffolk rector, she was the opposite of him, too. Her deeply-set, exhausted eyes and softly-delicate, non-games-playing hands and arms revealed the professional non-doer, who could somehow force people to scatter in order to do things for her. The mere thought of Clare, evoked by a letter from her, convinced one that her notepaper was scented, though in fact it wasn't.

Two husbands, who overlapped badly, both felt compelled, whatever the facts, to unload money for her.* She never had to ask. But what first struck one was the fearful perfectionism of Clare's home. She lived in West Suffolk ('it's in my blood,' she said faintly). 'William and Mary' would correctly describe some layer too deep seated to be conveniently revealed. Clare specialized on interiors: and the lack of dark ledges under which unseeworthy objects could be shoved with the foot, the finish of bedrooms, house accoutrements, tooth glass holders, was too absolute. Everything, even the central heating, was somehow lacquered. This foible did not by itself make Clare ridworthy. Some men liked it. Overdrive, to begin with, doted on it. It was only later that it induced in him a rigidity, a fear of breaking things, a nervousness in case cigarette ash was dropped even on the garden path, or a rug left with a

* 'moths round the candle', said Odoreida, who had a complete collection of the novels of Geoffrey Farnol. 'Mothsmanship', as a term of description of Clare's technique, is under consideration, although now *new* 'manship' words are double screened and triple inspected before adoption, and must not be used unless they bear the Yeovil imprint.

suggestion of a ruck. One did long for dust, if not mud. It was impossible to drop anything in Clare's house. Personal odds and ends were immediately sucked into a cupboard, itself gleaming with new paint and dusted up to the almost invisible top. Overdrive began to dread the sight of Merritt, Clare's manservant, laying out, with special precision, his dark trousers which had the blindingly shiny patch on the left side of the seat. He began to think that Merritt was getting at him. The heavy carpeting of the ground floor seemed to erupt beyond the confines of the porches to the very doors of the stable. One's least dented cigarette lighter or only clean pair of pants looked shabby, disintegrated, gangrenous. All was chosen: nothing accrued. Fruit was selected to go with the plates, and lighting arranged to emphasize the fruit contours. In the bathroom, the colour of the toilet paper, laid out in a tray in a fan, blank, like a bad bridge hand, matched the wall of the bathroom. Overdrive began to dream that he had seen Persian carpet in the cowshed.

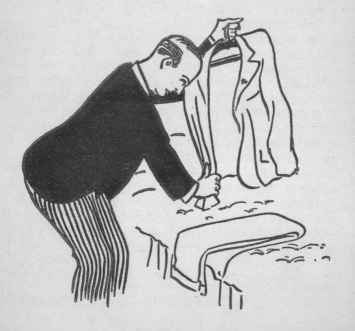

The end came, for Overdrive, because he suffered from athlete's foot. Clare would occasionally peep into his bedroom to make sure that everything was safe. In fact, Gordon Overdrive was super careful, and even put down pieces of newspaper, no bad precaution, when he was going to brush his suit over the ivory white carpet. One day he was about to paint his toes with Fungifuge, the athlete's foot cure, when he heard Clare's hand on the latch. He quickly hid the bottle.

'What are you doing, Gordon?' Clare said.

He looked strange, sitting on the bed fully dressed but in bare feet.

'Oh, recueillering pour mieux sautering,' said Overdrive, attempting the meaninglessly witty.

'By the way, Gordon, why do you keep that extraordinary green bottle half hidden by the flowers on the dressing table?'

'Oh, that's for my athlete's foot,' said Overdrive, trying to make the complaint sound manly.

'Your *foot*?' said Clare.

'It's only a fungus, really. You see—'

'A fungus,' said Clare. 'How horrible. Do you mean—' Clare shrank back a little and forced herself to stare at Overdrive's toenails, which were thickish.

'You mustn't think in terms of toadstools of course,' said Overdrive, trying to cheer it up: but Clare, lifting the skirts of her robe a little seemed to be picking her way out of the room.

Alone again, Overdrive sat still. It was all absurd, of course. But why did he feel obscurely apprehensive?

Suddenly he knew. It was the cork. *The cork*. It was still in his hand—the stopper of the bottle of Fungifuge. He had forgotten to cork it. He felt behind him in the bed. There was a slight dampness. On the outer coverlet of old lace and muslin, the stain of green was not much larger than half a crown. But it was spreading, and the stain on the eiderdown was larger, and the stain on the blanket below, the satin edged blanket, was larger still. And below that—.

'And I suppose the carpet's ruined too—,' Overdrive said

out loud, in a strained voice: but already he was packing his bag. Thank heaven no chance of Merritt sarcastically folding that old pair of pants. He got out of the house without anybody hearing. He left a note, affectionate but dignified, saying 'all bills to me.' Probably at this moment he was at his best, because everybody knew there was no point in sending bills to Overdrive.*

Failure to Avoid Youth

Winkle was just 17, and Gattling thought every now and then that he should talk to her. She was obviously pretty

---

* We have so far said nothing of genuine life-counters to Clare, but a Freshman with us, little Tommy Pikkins, was made a full member by his plucky attempt to put Clare one down. His method—to fall in with her mind-the-carpets neurosis but *slightly overdo it*. For example he will keep taking out his handkerchief and polishing e.g., the already brilliantly shining top of the sugar tongs. 'Once you get pitting', he will say. Occasionally Clare herself will drop a spot of water when she is doing the house plants. 'Have you tried Jellicoe?' he will say, pretending to squeeze something out of a tube. He will wipe his feet when he is going out of the house as much as when he is coming in, and be found spraying the small bird's nest hidden above the garden door. 'Beware of spotted flycatcher's odour,' he will say. 'If one thought of the festering bodies of mutilated midges. . . .' To counter women who perpetually hover with ash trays, Pikkins produces one of his own, a discarded sardine tin. Alternatively, he drops ash ostentatiously in his turn-ups (N. Viney's ploy).

but it was difficult to see her, sometimes, as she was always sitting about on couches with a magazine for older women on the floor in front of her which she read bent double, her face concealed by her hair, which hung in front of her face. She looked so slender and light he could have picked her up with one hand. So Gattling told us. When he came in to talk to her Gattling found himself hesitating a moment outside the door. He walked in slightly sideways.

'Hail, Winkle,' he said, rather as if she was twelve. Be natural, he said to himself.

'Oh, hallo,' Winkle said, turning a page.

'She gets that drawl from her mother,' thought Gattling.

Winkle bent a little lower over a large photograph of Charles Boyer. She had heard her mother mention this name, seemingly with respect. Her hair just touched the ground.

'All well?' said Gattling.

'Oh—no too bad. You know?'

Whenever she spoke to him she turned another page of the mag. with a crisp snap.

'Is *he* a good man?' Gattling had now gone over to the pile of gramophone discs and picked one up. On the sleeve was a coloured photograph of a fairly young boy with aggressive dimples, a dent chopped out of his chin, pink cheeks, and an absolutely white nose.

'You don't hear about him much now,' she said.

'I can imagine he could pall,' said Gattling. He had always hoped this girl would get on to something better. He held the photograph at arm's length.

'Is he—well, is he—'

Turning another page, Winkle cut him short. 'I don't think he was ever a queer,' she said, believing that to Gattling this was the first step, the first division, in the classifying of mankind. 'Are they dicotoledon or homocotyledon?' she would say, making fun of Gattling and her old botany mistress at the same time. We realized—I realized —she thought them not unalike. Gattling was surprised but pleased to be talking with Winkle on such modern terms.

Obviously his method was right. 'I expect he's awfully good,' he began.

'He likes Beethoven,' said Winkle, referring to a second main category in Gattling's assessments. He *had* thought of introducing the subject of something easy but good, like Elgar's violin concerto.

'Rather glad your friends don't look like him,' Gattling-Fenn said jerkily. Winkle had just picked up a postcard from a friend, and Gattling, trying to read it too, saw that it started 'Hi, spastic!'

'Oh, they wouldn't. They're mags, you see, not maggers.' Winkle brightened up. She liked explaining the words.*

'You mean the girls don't wear those toeless boots?' said Gattling, after the explanation.

'Oh yes they wear boots—sort of—but always long skirts at night. And we do have our hair cut we really do.'

'Of course I think the twist is first class, as a dance.' Gattling had been saying this for years.

'How's twisting?'

'Well, there's a thing called the Wallop now you know? Or the Hoodoo . . . you probably know? It's sort of *trad* twist, I suppose.'

'But surely they still dance the twist at the "Fetlock Room"?' said Gattling as if he was producing a trump card.

'Yes—that's right' said Winkle. 'You'll like that. It's fairly empty these days . . . and there's lots of older people.'

'Good,' said Gattling, making dummy twist motions. But actually, to my eye, he had been led perilously near to a woo situation; and now old sores were beginning to ooze on his breastbone, and from the weals across his forehead a drop of blood began to form.

STUDENT: Is there a counter to the great youth gambit, the one-upness of being young?

OLD LIFEMAN: Emphatically. Be old. As old as possible.

* This conversation took place way back in 1967.

If necessary be wheeled into the room in a bath chair.
But never, whatever you do, be, if old, young.

Danger of Competence, in Women

'Poor old Overdrive', said Gozzler. 'It's always the same.
The situation's hopeless if the woman hasn't got a job.'

'Hope—' we started indistinctly, as if echoing: but we*
weren't sure if the hopelessness was finally proved, nor
had we finally decided which line to take.

'How about—' we began: but Gozzler was able to in-
terrupt so near to instantaneously that the speaker often
apologized for interrupting *him*.

'Thank God they all do something nowadays. It gives
them a shape. It gives them a surface.'

Gozzler's surface was as exact as a nut, and almost
everything he said was so clear that it made your mind
wander. Gozzler was of course quite high in the Home
Office: but though I have read a dozen times his rather
long entry in *Who's Who,* it somehow bounces off the
eye. 'Deputy Regional Commissioner Reconstruction and

* See Dictionary. 'We' means 'I', but it is more nicechap and far less
egotistical.

Grade Supply' is the most vividly descriptive sentence. ('Grade' brings it to life, said Gattling.)

'Yes, do you know Barbara Wick?' Gozzler said looking serious.

'Yes we do.'

'Well she is working for me now.'

Gozzler smiled rather more than he meant to; and at once we scented a woo situation. Wick illustrated the truism that clarity in women is more potent than clarity in men. Their skin and fingers and footwear are better adapted to express it. This kind of psycho-physical distinctness is often attractive, and some men feel calmed down and tidied up merely by being in the presence of precision. Gozzler himself was perfectly clear cut down to the Adam's apple: below he was a hive of swarming doubts in a chaos of cul-de-sacs.

Wick was attractive, or at any rate, with her deep set grey eyes, straight nose and good keen line of the jaw she

According to Wiratz, 'there is one moment, which may only last 1.5 seconds, when, in the relationship between two P.A.S.s, neither is one-up on the other.'

could with scarcely a suggestion of back-handing be called handsome. Her face was a clear print of a face. Gozzler felt he needed her.

We could have warned Gozzler but we knew he'd find out for himself and he did. It was the third time they had met outside their work. Alban Gozzler liked to give little bridge foursome dinners in his flat. He had read a novel, the hero of which was described as carving a bird with 'clean, deft motions'. Alban was not quite up to this, but when he was about to take the wing off the duck he was astonished to hear a voice from the table.

'No—excuse me—start nearer the breast?' It was Wick. There was a pause. He tried to visualize what must have been a bizarre scene at the table, behind his back. Suddenly he realized she was referring to his carving. 'A-*ha*!' Alban said lightly, but he did not feel light. Afterwards, playing bridge with Wick his partner, he started off with the usual: 'Two clubs—and no-trump strongish?'

'You tell me what you want to play and I'll play it, partner.' Wick's smile emphasized the chilling one-upness of this remark.

P.A.S.-ing

But it was a long time before Gozzler could find anything definite to kick against. Sometimes Wick rattled him by her silences, when he was making an interesting point. If anybody disagreed with him she would laugh suddenly in a brief snort, as if she had been trying not to. Whose side was she on?

As a passenger in his car she was too sophisticated to be a back-seat driver, yet she had a way of studying some document while he was driving her, as if she couldn't bear to look out of the window.

One evening (Alban told me after) when Wick was looking particularly attractive and, for her, mildly feminine, he called to drive her to the Haymarket Theatre. She asked him if he would like to go 'by her special way'.

'Tell me dear lady,' Gozzler said.

Afterwards, starting off for a St. James's Street restaurant, she said 'Of course you do know that Pall Mall is a one way street now?' Gozzler was silent, but the pigeons rose in unison from the eaves of the Haymarket Theatre.

When he didn't reply, Wick was not rebuffed but added quietly and clearly 'One way Going *West.*'

'Don't you see what she's doing?' we said to Gozzler, whose chief thing, in a sense, was knowing Clubs, and who could therefore find his way round this particular section under near total anaesthetic.

'Which is doing what?' said Alban, trying to keep on top of the dialogue.

'Wick. She's P.A.S.-ing you.'

'Funny wordies?' Alban was resisting.

'Just because she's going to be a Principal Assistant

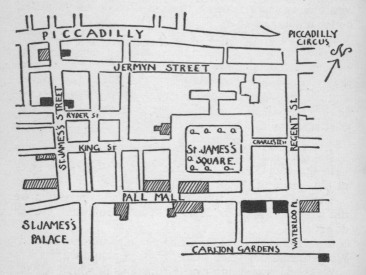

Sketch map of the basic club area ('Gozzler's Terrain'). Shaded blocks show clubs from which Gattling-Fenn, by contrast, has been blackballed: filled-in blocks show those which he is not allowed to enter even as a guest.

Secretary, she's Principally Assisting you all round the compass. Just because last year she showed an unexpected grasp of the effect of monopolies on the deaf-aid industry —she thinks she can therefore clarify everybody's thoughts on all subjects, from abstract American painting to the topography of Boodles, with the technique of manipulating a small dinghy on the Hamble thrown in.'

In the end our efforts prevailed and Gozzler had to admit that Wick was not the woman for him. Shortly afterwards he resigned from the Civil Service, leaving Wick to clarify all her rivals into a state of confusion, and to break all previous records of smooth promotion for Cambridge educated Home Office women.

Gozzler's overt reason for leaving Wick was that he wanted to write. (If pressed he would say that he felt he ought to put on record that period, in '44, when he was 'the man in the corner, taking notes'). I believe the fact was that he knew it was 6 to 4 on Wick being promoted on top of him.

But he never got clear of Wick, though he became engaged to Pickering. Pickering had large soft eyes. She was endearing, like a child. 'Pretty child,' Wick said of her, after Gozzler had produced her. Gozzler kept his temper.

Pickering slightly clung to Gozzler when she spoke to him: Wick looked at her with clear-eyed interest, as if she was adjusting the lens to f16 in order to photograph a Ngambian fertility dance.

'But she's charming.'

In the end Gozzler separated from Pickering, in spite of the appeal of her wet looking eyelashes.

Gozzler and Wick were united after all. Even then we did not desert him. He came to us in a somewhat 'broken down' state.

'For God's sake give me a Lifemanship counter,' he said. We gave him our small mimeographed pamphlet.*

We even created anti-clarity situations in which Alban, after an hour of looking vague, might suddenly dart in and correct Wick on a point of fundamental detail.

'No,' he was able to say at one pre-arranged point,

* 'How to be Right about Facts: or You May Very Well Be Correct, But'.

though Wick was putting him off by appearing to be engaged in some sort of needlework. 'The standard of living index has risen in Mexico since 1950 to 44.'

But Wick simply bent her neck over her gros point and said 'Did you get those figures from the 1965 Corbett's?'

Whether or not she was making up this name it was impossible for us to tell. Actually we got ours from a 1951 Whitaker's.

Two years later we could see that Wick and Gozzler were once more on the point of breaking. In the H.O. Wick was already one rank over Gozzler's all-time high, and she was preparing a definitive Report: Gozzler had only got up to chapter eight of his book. He had changed the title from *Thoughts and Memoirs of an Assistant Under-Commissioner* to *Crisis in Camera,* which he believed would give him a pretty certain chance of Sunday paper serialisation.

Wick agreed so warmly to the new title that Alban gave her the MS of his chapter eight. But a day passed, and no comment. *Nothing whatever.* Next morning, Alban had to ask her:

GOZZLER: Did you look at that stuff?

WICK *(almost instantly stifling an instantaneous yawn which yet slightly affected the pronunciation of her first word):* Yes I *did.*

GOZZLER: O.K.?

WICK: Most amusing.

GOZZLER: Amusing? Oh you mean that bit about *Mc-Andrew,* which of course is MacAlpine. Do you think Mac will get me for libel?

WICK: Libel? Oh good heaven's no. It's awfully nice.

GOZZLER: Nice?

The end came, in so far as there was an end, over Wick's report. One day Wick said: 'I'm going to work in the morning room.'

GOZZLER: You won't disturb me.

WICK: No, I know. But I've got to be alone doing the stuff.

The frightful implication, by Wick, that she was the real writer, finally had its effect.

'Me too!' said Alban in a raised voice, and this went straight into our Black Book of Unrecommended Retorts.*

The perfect parallel to Wick is Angus Ballock, married to Arnold Ballock, the composer. The sight even of blank music paper made her yawn continuously, on a high pitched note, at half minute intervals.

Garda's Outside Man

We celebrated the final separation of Wick and Gozzler. I had managed to get special invited audience tickets for the new B.B.C. panel game *One Over the Seven,* and we followed this by whiskies, off I.T., in my apartment. I noticed, then, a change in Alban. He still wanted to be definite and clear, but was dead off home government. He now took evening classes at the Tufton Park School of Sculpture, did some painting, and was especially interested in the drama,† though he took little notice of the B.B.C. show. He wore looser, more artistic clothes, with a ramshackle tie; though he was never quite able to let go. The haphazard effect seemed to have been sprayed with some fixative, so that it never varied.

Alban made references to 'Garda'. We knew her as a long thin dark woman who, had she lived in the eighteen fifties, would certainly have had a pre-Raphaelite neck.

'What I want,' said Gozzler, 'is somebody to whom I can talk. Simple and natural freedom *without feeling that I have sold my integrity and the rights of my own separate world.'*

'What he meant was somebody he could boss and who wouldn't boss back,' Coad said. He was inclined to give up Gozzler altogether.

And yet in our position as preservers of the status woo quo, I felt I ought to say to Alban, with a look:

* cf. 'Oh no I'm not' as a reply to 'Aren't you a tremendous specialist in Wagner?'

†He was a 'Friend of Chichester', which made it possible for him to see the 1967 *Othello,* when the name part was to be acted by a Negro playing it as a white man made up as a Moor.

'You've heard, of course, of Dr Busardi.'

He hadn't: but my mind went back ten years to little Pip Pennycuick, who had also thought he had found someone he could talk to, and perhaps help, in Garda, who was then only thirty-three herself. Pip was impressed by the furniture and pictures of her room, almost every item of which could be called early. She had just picked up an early Mondrian, which must have been painted almost in infancy. Pip conceived that she was interested in him because as a new-made graduate writing a thesis for his B.Litt., he could be a teacher and guide to her. She was certainly a splendid listener; when she turned her head to pay attention it was like being caught in the beams from a distant lighthouse, gentle yet clear. Pip, having taken his degree in Eng. Lit., thought he could talk with special authority on Dostoievsky and Lawrence, Camus and Kafka.

All went well till Pip went one stage further and began to speak to her of the mystical side of Dostoievsky, and the *experience-philosophy* as he called it (or thought he had) of Blake and Melville. He was gaining ground. Then one day she said

'Some time, I must bring you to see Dr Busardi.'

'Dr Busardi?'

'You won't know even his name. But I think it would be good—' Garda turned the lighthouse full on him.

'I'd love to see him.'

'Well, it isn't quite like that, I mean not quite easy. It's something that's got to be arranged.'

Pip began to feel uneasy. 'Is he some sort of psychologist?' he said. Garda's laugh was as free and uninhibited as her smile. Pip did not like the way things were going.

'Far from it. He hates words like that.'

'You mean, perhaps, that he understands that we are each of us separate worlds, to be bridged?'

Pip was trying to get back; but Garda made no reply, and seemed to be thinking of something else.

I knew then, as I know now, that Garda would always bring in this Dr Busardi, and that Gozzler would never get to meet him, and that then things would come to a dead stop. I knew then, that Dr Busardi was pear-shaped

and shinily bald, and that he had written a book on the
'philosophy of self-realization.' I have never had any reason to believe that Dr Busardi was a fraud. I only remember meaning to tell Garda, which I never did, that I thanked
God I was not in his clutches. And I did not want Gozzler
to find himself getting bad life marks for frustration.

These are only about half—say 58%—of the types which
men who are approaching the orbit of woo should learn to
recognize clearly. We advocate independence of action.
Let them judge for themselves whether progress towards
the ultimate and inevitable goal should not be superceded
by an evocation of the discriminatory processes of objectivity.*

---

* Note to our Swedish Translator: Do not attempt to simplify this
sentence. Polysyllabic writing is part of our campaign to purify English
of the short simple Saxon words, except of course for those who want
to be short simple and Saxon.

3

Warnings for Women

Except for Ivy Spring (*One-Upmanship* p. 88), our staff is strongest on the male side. Yet the essence of Lifemanship is fairness. It is for this reason therefore, and no other, that now we have demonstrated the woo dangers in women, we intend to suggest that there have been proved to exist certain kinds of men with whom any question of a response to a woo should prompt a harrowing re-assessment.*

* 'harrowing re-assessment' is our new synonym for 'second thoughts' ('Agonizing re-appraisal' no longer O.K.).

On First Sight

'Some men are putting-off at first sight' said the Very Old Lifeman to the Newly Qualified.

N.Q.: Is this due to some physical blemish?

V.O.L.: (*deepening his perpetual smile*): Not necessarily.

N.Q.: To age perhaps—the man might be frightfully old?

V.O.L.: (*taking out a pocket comb*): Not necessarily. In men these things are not important.

N.Q.: What is?

V.O.L: (*combing his whitish beard outward from the nicotine-stained hole in the middle*): One must not be personally unattractive.

N.Q.: (*firming up, momentarily*): One must be clean, obviously.

V.O.L.: Clean *looking*. But it depends on the profession. The soil of work, manly mud, can look refreshingly clean. But if one has made the basic though corrigible life-mistake of working in an office in a city, perpetual *seeming* cleanliness is essential. Have one work shirt which you can wear for a fortnight: but for business lunches* a drawer full of blindingly white new shirts which can quickly be substituted. The slightest greyness suggests constant employment under the eaves of a railway terminus.

N.Q.: How about something on the hair?

V.O.L.: Some old men like to lean forward suddenly and give women an unexpected whiff of something. We used to do this in 1904. Others spend hours trying to smell of nothing whatever. It's a difficult question. Personally I use a tested beard deodorant. Superficial cleanliness is the important thing, and it is especially important when it overcomes environment.

N.Q.: What about—well—cosmetics really—for men?

* After a lot of ditherings, the Director of the Spoken Life now finally discards 'luncheon' in favour of the more democratic, slightly left-wing 'lunch'.

Surely . . . I mean I use talcum powder—sometimes it happens to be slightly scented I know but. . . .

v.o.l.: Steady. You've got the right approach I think. In the all-in wrestling championship we are against providing seconds with scent sprays. In other circumstances, though, it all depends on what you call it. Manufacturers of 'Old Stewed Steak for Men' or 'General Jackson's Depilator' don't go far enough in their emphasis on virility. 'Pentathlon', 'Miner's Cap', and 'Four-Minute Mile' are patented, as names, by us, of cover-whiffs for the busy man unable fully to wash. The important thing is to overcome circumstances.

n.q.: Can you give me any more examples, sir?

v.o.l.: Yes. If you have just driven a car 400 miles through the Potteries and the Black Country in the rain with a leaky roof and had a puncture in the Pennines, you should be able to step out in front of your Scottish hostess with properly ironed trousers.

n.q.: But how. . . .

v.o.l.: Creased in the front, creased in the rear. If the necessity is absolute the method will come. One can always change trousers at the lodge gates.

n.q.: Is there no alternative?

v.o.l.: As always, in Lifemanship, the alternative is equally good. Be the opposite. If rival is expert crease-man, wear jeans. Tie the tie, if any, actually round the neck, missing collar altogether. But be one thing or the other. Beware of un-self-consciousness.

n.q.: You mean self-consciousness?

At this point v.o.l. gets as near to stopping smiling as he can and speaks in a voice which crackles like a sodium flare (the 'Bertrand Russell rational').

v.o.l.: Self-conscious. Know what you are doing before you do it so that you know you are doing what you are doing.

We have recorded this conversation in full not because

it is typical of two old Harrovians but in order to help women to cross off a few men before they have even opened their mouths.

On First Acquaintance

Women are quicker than men at recognizing unwoo-worthiness in the opposite sex. They are less affected by outward appearance. They know from internal evidence that beauty and handsomeness, so far from being only skin deep, permeate the whole character. Good looks are a primary one-upness in human relationships, and create a personal confidence and composure, in company, which will compare badly with their effectiveness in more private and less romantic circumstances. Contrary to the sentiments of the poem, when pain and anguish wring the brow that kind of coy beauty woman will probably turn up Beta Minus. Still fewer are the examples of men with a clear cut one-two-three profile who can be relied on to climb three flights of stairs with a glass of warm milk.

Deep Voice.
Not looks, then, but behaviour. Women will quickly recognize the warning sign of Deep Voice. It will go on, morning or late, always deep, always confident, at the same level tempo whether ordering drinks or sympathizing with news of the death of a beloved old governess.

Small Smile.
An English version of deepness includes Small Smile, who ends almost every conversation sequence with an only just observable pluck on a chord of some emotion felt exclusively by smiler.

'He was always very good to *me*.' (Small smile.)
Or

'Of course we all backed him up. Rather naturally, we were glad of the chance.' (Small smile.)

There is often the threat of humour in his voice.

'Aha—cue for my exit, isn't it?' (Exits, with small smile.)

On First Signs of Woo: Indistinctness a Danger Signal

Here we plunge straight into a major contra-indication of woo, and one which divides the sexes with a scimitar. Men quite like to meet men and women who are indistinct in character. It gives them confidence. But women, unless they are dyed in the grain maternalists, do not like it, and should regard vagueness as a major contra-indication.

An exaggerated instance of this is young Cuffey, of whom it is inaccurate to say that women found him difficult even to see because in fact he was to them, to start with, completely invisible. Even at quite a small drink gathering, Cuffey was never noticed. When a fine young woman passed him or indeed when she was introduced to him it was like a wave breaking over his head. He almost immediately found himself obliterated in the trough of her wake, forgotten and unnoticed. By the time he had said 'haven't we met before' this great beacon of a girl was already in the middle of a new group.

'Talking to yourself?' said Coad. Coad and I were inclined to slap Cuffey teasingly on the back.

'You must be more definite,' I said. 'Say "Weren't you the girl who was elected *Reine des Fleurs* at Le Touquet?"' The girl will like this, especially if she has never been nearer to France than Angmering. Try it. 'Weren't you the girl. . . .'

Cuffey is quiet but he is persistent. And 18 months after this advice, and after practising this phrase and getting quite good tuition on the unidiomatic 'Reine des Fleurs', he found himself one day in Victoria Station, in a Crystal Palace train, sitting opposite a girl so appallingly pretty, with mobile soft lower lip, thick locks of chestnut hair falling to her shoulders, and eyes lowered to display toothbrush-thick eyelashes, that Cuffey determined at once to put his phrase into operation.

Unfortunately, while he was having one silent runthrough, a woman, obviously the girl's mother, came in and sat down beside the girl and started talking. Nevertheless it did seem to Cuffey that the girl had glanced at him. And, listening to their conversation, he heard Eyelash tell her mother that she was going to have a golf lesson at the Merton Golf Club on the following Monday.

Cuffey had not heard of this Club, but he turned up that morning, and after walking sideways towards Eyelash, with a strange gait, he yet made his recommended remark (stumbling a little over 'weren't you the girl'— he said 'wasn't') and we were all glad to hear *it was a complete success,* and well followed up by Cuffey, who

achieved a meeting at the Piccadilly Hotel, where he had once seen the words 'dinner-dance' advertised in the lobby.

All this was in Cuffey's earliest years—date, about 1920, when the phrase 'dinner-dance' had remarkable prestige. But nothing can soften the hard facts of the sequel, the sequence of which was fully confessed by Cuffey two years later. The dinner had gone well, until the actual paying of the bill, which Cuffey for some reason asked for by saying in a high clear voice 'Can I have the bill, please', which of course was not too good. Then, as he later told us, in the taxi to Hammersmith, Eyelash looked more anguishingly pretty than ever. His mother wouldn't have approved of all that make-up. Had she intensified it when she got her cloak? Tremendously, he believed. It frightened him. His heart sank. The taxi would have to dodder along for twenty minutes before it reached Carlyon Road, Hammersmith. Silence fell. Now, he knew, we all would say that he ought to kiss her. He wanted to kiss her. Surely she would—he had almost said 'should' to himself, and even that ghost of a caddish thought made him despise himself, and lowered the temperature. Where now was his confident gaiety which he had been able to

assume when he said 'Weren't you the girl?' Horrors—
the gloomy arches of Olympia, all lights out, were already
approaching. Now he must say it—'Will you kiss me?'

Why was she disappearing, as it were, down some long
corridor? What had happened? What was it? Where was
he? Where was she?

Aids to the Envisagement of Post-Marital Behaviour-Deterioration

It would have been easy to predict the later life of Cuffey,
in spite of the unexpected and quite enterprising course
of his career. He interpreted our advice to 'be something'
as a hint that he should develop his interest in the theatre. Coad, who was up Grants with him at Westminster
School, used to quote their housemaster's saying that 'Cuffey was probably the best Cinna in the history of amateur
Julius Caesar'. It wasn't till 1940 that we realized that
Cinna only had eight words to say.

But long before that we had observed Cuffey continuing
to fail, on the actual woman front. I remember hearing
him ask the beautifully slender Loretta, four inches taller
than Cuffey, to go out with him.

'And we might, sort of, dance?' Cuffey said. Quite
charming, but to the girl's horror, to her deep and barely
concealed loathing, he added

'Tell me, where would you like to go?'

Needless to say he lost Loretta.* Later he became attracted to a widow, a Mrs Gell. He made a real effort
to take a strong line, and I was actually present when,
unprompted, he made a remark which caused me to clap
my hands invisibly under the table.

'I would take that child away from that school at once.

* This was not a question of difference in height. Loretta was nearly a
foot taller than Odoreida, who liked her but was the world record issuer
of unattractive invitations to women. 'Go to Il Pescados at 6.45' he would
say. 'It's two floors up the building behind the bomb site in Carey Wharf
Street, five minutes from the Aldgate East tube. Half hidden by an ad-
vertisement for Chlorodyne. You can't miss it. And if I'm late buy yourself drinks.'

A convent is quite wrong for her anyway.' Good for Cuffey.

He said this with great definiteness. His features are a little too small for this remark but the effect was good. Yet the mere fact that people seemed suddenly to be taking his word for gospel made him nervous. His features became screwed up in a bundle in the middle of his face.

'Don't,' I said involuntarily, realizing he was going to re-examine his decision. Sure as fate came

'At the end of the term anyway.'

There was a lowering of pulse-rates. A minute later he was saying 'Provided of course there is somewhere really *good* for her to go to'. Before long he was actually trying to go into reverse, with:

'Of course we ought to ask her, I suppose, what she really wants—don't you think?' Needless to say, he lost Monica Gell.

Cuffey did become more positive in other fields. He was a member of Lloyds, but looked much better in his world-of-the-theatre clothes, when, wearing corduroy trousers and almost unbelievably woolly pullovers, he seemed nearly twice the size.

But Cuffey was his own warning. He continued to fall down flat with women. He did actually make some progress in the theatre, and, as a producer of professionals, I saw him rehearsing a Sunday performance, for the Players Group, of *Father Future* from East Germany. He had had the, to me, incredible luck of getting hold of the wondrous Madame Elsa for the principal part: yet I couldn't help realizing, at the first read-through, that she saw the sort of man he was. Those ginger tweeds and black shirt, that late arrival, that sudden boy-like sitting on the ground at her feet, the use of completely inappropriate words to suggest atmosphere. All personality and no person.

'This scene must be played in a phosphorescent light, psychologically. The penthouse is, emotionally, beneath the surface of the sea.'

La Elsa refused to respond to this. Had she perhaps guessed that he was the sort of producer who, where a known actress was concerned, would be much more talkative at the read-through than at any other period in the production? That in fact the chief rehearsing he would do, after a good drink based on Pernaud, would be of himself, alone, before the read-through started?

Suddenly sitting on the edge of the table, Cuffey thrust his long dank locks very near the almost international Elsa. Although he was half bald, one was conscious at the same time that he had a lot of hair.

'But . . . suppose I can too. . . .'
Cuffey was reading a rather uninteresting cue in Act II.

'That is your first realization. First hint—something new in tone. Your voice takes on a different note—has *foresight* in it. A cloud, no bigger than. . . .'

Cuffey would actually continue for two full minutes on the subject of this moment of the scene. When he had finished, Elsa did not smile or speak. She took her elegant, thin blue pencil, and made a dot on her script somewhere near this line, half missing it, and turned to somebody else to talk about something else. Needless to say, he never got any further with La Elsa.

Our Short List of Danger Signals for Women

We have examined the case of Cuffey in a little detail because it emphasizes a primal tenet of our anti-woo approach. Men, but particularly women (to whom we are especially talking in this chapter, although so often male is female and vice versa) should, if brought within the range of a Possible (if Probable the 'should' becomes 'must') try to see the woo object as he or she might develop on longer acquaintance, particularly on longer married acquaintance. In the bow-and-arrows age of the 'Twenties I remember that the man was advised to look carefully at the mother-in-law, for a sign which was often a warning. No need to point out that in 1965 the mother-in-law is likely to look as sympathetic, slightly more soignée, and decidedly younger than her daughter; so that this rule no longer holds.

At the same time, for women, there are certain signs, portents, which with our help the careful woman may be able to interpret and judge. Is the admirable characteristic natural, she must ask. Or is he keeping up by a tremendous effort some trait which, with a sigh of relief, he may, after marriage, discard or even substitute by the opposite?

Well Turned Out.
On these first meetings what attracts you to him may be the result of gymnastics in the bathroom. There has been the check-up on nails, shaving down to the base of the jugulars; the wearing of at least an occasional new garment, attention to clean socks, reasonable odour, stomach muscle exercises never forgotten, deep breathing when standing in a queue. Is he going to be as trim fourteen dates later? If there is the slightest falling off, beware the possibilities of change in two years time. The general switch, perhaps, from junior to senior: the making of a very slight meal of being older than he is. The morning throat clearing a shade more fruity than necessary. Irritating little toothpaste residues in the bathroom. A pre-

liminary wheeze to tune up, then off we go into the morning cough of an extrovert nature.

Angle of Gaze.
Watch his eye, too. Watch to see that when it is looking at you he is looking at you. Remember that by a slight shift of focus, the loving glance can turn into an absent stare over your left shoulder.

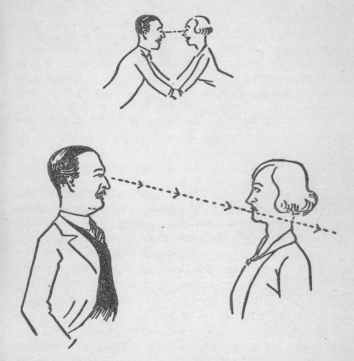

Sense of Occasion.
Has he, by amusing chance, thought that *Giovanni* instead of the *Magic Flute* was your first opera together (last summer, it was)? Then remember that it is quite possible that after marriage, the dialogue will go like this:

  WOMAN: (*driving the car*): What does that funny red clock tower remind you of?

MAN: (*smiling but thinking hard*): You mean the *tower*?

WOMAN: The tower.

MAN: Well, it's rather like Glasgow Central station as a matter of fact (*begins cautious laugh*).

WOMAN: Is it? No, I only meant we used to see it from Virginia Water.

MAN: *Yes,* my god. My *god*.

Ear for Music.

In other words watch his sense of occasion. Going to the opera together, for instance, should include a back reference, however slight, to the fact that once upon a time he fingered out opera themes* beforehand, on the piano, while she wrote out a version of the plot in super synopsisese. Fits of uncontrollable laughter.

How will the fits of laughter department be in two years time?

Ear for listening.

Does he listen?

In these early weeks the thought can be half spoken and yet it comes clear over the love-wave intercom. Some day the effect may be different: perhaps even somebody may be not quite listening.

True the longer you know each other the more you will have in common. But there still may come a period when the invitations happen to have run out and you find yourselves boxed up alone for the evening meal for the tenth day running. And you will note that his eyes are not starting out of his head when you are telling him your prime story of the day, about Gwen Chevening and the coloured trumpeter.

WOMAN: You don't answer.

MAN: (*looking keen*): Fancy! Mrs Chevening.

WOMAN: That's Adela Chevening, she's sixty-eight. I was talking about Gwen.

* Women if they wish can widen any incipient rift by an exaggerated display of what is known as This was Our Tunemanship.

MAN: I'm sorry, I couldn't hear.

WOMAN: You're not listening.

MAN: My darling, I was struggling with all my might. I even stopped eating my cheese biscuit when I saw you were going to speak.

WOMAN: One does get deafer. . . .

MAN: Sometimes I only know you're speaking because your lips are moving. . . .

WOMAN: You must see by radar. You were staring at the newspaper.

MAN: (*beginning to assume wronged voice*): Well. You did ask me to find a movie. But even if you're in a different *room* you go on talking to me sometimes, without in the slightest raising your voice.*

(*Silence*)

Warning

Women in danger of Woo must beware of men who show signs of trying to counteract creeping vagueness by a sort of penny-in-the-slot politeness, a Jack-in-the-box opening of doors. The prognosis for this is bleak. Solicitous attentiveness, while the man is actually thinking about Kempton Park or internally humming, *pom*-pom, the last movement of Bach's Italian concerto, may develop into an even slightly sarcastic 'deep' gaze, chin supported on elbow. Alternatively the man may suddenly reveal himself in the guise of a great believer in separate worlds. He may forget what he has said in the past about exchange of interests, and the pleasure of making the bridge between two identities. Or he may tend to limit his outside pursuits to one of the five unalterably non-women subjects, the latest accredited list of which, nicknamed the 'Five Es', are as follows:

* We are dealing, here, with Hake's Law—the rule, first formulated by Hake, and first described by him in his paper on 'Long-term Association and Geometrically Progressive Inaudibility'. This is Gamesman A.N.C. Hake who won the Sunderland Evening News Golf Competition by returning a net 58 off a handicap of 32.

Entomology
Etymology
Egyptology
Echology and
EGANDS*

Characteristicness

'How typical' the woman in danger of woo may say of
her rather fascinating recent acquaintance.

She should remember that in some men marriage acts
as a sort of fertilizer of their eccentricities. Fixed character
traits, instead of being washed away, seem to stand out
in relief.

A sensible system of filing letters may turn into a mania
for keeping the envelopes as well, together with old numbers of St Mark's Parish Magazine, jelly-graphed wine
lists of the Bottoms Up Club, or the Ten Pin Bowling
Gazette. There will be a special drawer full of used camera films long past the latest possible date when they

* Word formed from the initials of the phrase 'Explanation of the Geo-
logical Association between North Downs and South'. The fireside conversation of Gattling-Fenn, I remember, in the tenth year of his second
marriage, had become almost exclusively Egands.

ought to be developed. After his divorce, the bottom cupboard of Odoreida's wardrobe was found to be full of empty bottles of his hair tonic with the date, recorded on the cap, when he had finished them.

The man who once took a double First behaves more and more exclusively as if he should take the double Top in conversation. He demonstrates, because he is the only person in the house who knows the correct position for the semi-colon, that he has the right to decide all problems from flower arrangement to things worth preserving architecturally.

The man who once got reasonable fun out of playing games develops fits of exercise mania. Suddenly he will become a before-breakfast bicyclist, a semi-dieter, or a corrective-neck-exercise man. He may even read a Manual of Home Nursing.

A man who as a youth was 'mad on cars', becomes truly mad, when this trait outlives its appropriateness. *His* car, *his* model, is the only movable object worth mentioning, even if it spends half of its life on tow. When he is teaching his wife to drive and she asks him how the clutch works, he clears decks and starts really to tell her how the clutch works while she is only longing for him to say something like 'put your foot down'.

'Imagine a pair of revolving cymbals being clasped slowly together,' he says.

'Yes?' says his wife.

'Well, that's it,' he says. 'Look, watch my hands. Now, the palms are coming closer and closer together . . . one of my hands is turning round.'

'Is it?' says his wife, looking hard.

'Well of course it can't really turn round.'

'I thought not.'

'I mean my hand can't turn round.'

There is a lack of give and take. In the same way the man who had the subsidiary merit and decent advantage of having been at Eton or Mag. Coll., Oxford, or a member of White's, or of the Guard's Club, becomes after marriage more bound to these institutions than ever, as if this was the principal thing about him and soon it is.

A sadly nostalgic picture for some of us. Mrs Godfrey
Plaste, wife of our late expert in carmanship, listens
while her husband explains the working of the clutch.

and in the end all you see is an OE tie isolated like a
tavern sign on a pub.

The man who, before marriage, was warmly, simply
and naturally in love, may become after marriage a terri-
fying sex expert. Or alternatively he is, sometimes Freudy-
weudy about it, or itsy bitzy tootsy about it, or he reads
large plain Gollanczy books about it to prove it is sane
and healthy and formative. Watch for first signs of this.

Watch also the man who confuses being a man, with
being manly. This is very often obvious in the wooing
period. The young man will be surprisingly in charge at
the ticket office, with the taxi driver, or with the waiter,
whom he will summon imperiously, perhaps trying to dis-
guise a youthful lack of personality. He will ask for wine
with stunning authority, have a slight quarrel with the
waiter, and then make it up with him good humouredly
at the end of the meal.

Much more serious may be an intensification of a need
to be manly later in marriage. If anything of seriousness
happens of a news kind, or of minor importance in the
house, then comes the pronouncement. The slightly slower
speech, the firmness, which you will first find lovable, then
funny, then boring, then just background noises.

A fatal possible addition is to try to be, to the children, not only father but A Father as well—wrong because impossible and leading to mistimed decisiveness and the inappropriate No.

Somewhere in the Bible, in Judges or Second Samuel, there is, or should be, the sentence

'Be not a lion in thine house.'

Remember that being associated with a lion is an operable disease, if taken early.

Wrong method of suggesting man of action used to dealing with large bodies of men.

4

Avoidance Gambits

Learning from Women

Why is it that as yet no volume has been written about
Lifemanship and Women? For the same reason that no
book has been written about *Gamesmanship and Cricket*.
Because just as all cricket *is* gamesmanship* so are all
women natural lifewomen.

* Contrast football, where accredited gamesmanship tactics are rare.
All the more deplorable therefore that *unsporting* behaviour in football is
often called 'gamesmanship' in the press by correspondents who have
never read our manuals.

Men who want to remain one-up on women should learn from them the art of one-up disassociation. 'Never argue with a woman', is insipid old folklore, one thinks, as one has a quick practice run-through of a few fairly unanswerable phrases. But thinking in terms of 'unanswerable' suggests already that the battle is going to be lost. Try:

'Of course if you'd rather go to watch Chelsea play *next* Saturday, let's do that instead.'

What will be the female answer?

'It's not a question of this Saturday or next Saturday. Why should it always be you choosing?'

Better to keep silent. Over a question of fact, if you humour the woman she will at once repeat 'Just as you say dear', as if it were she who was doing the humouring. If as a move towards placation, or out of some real largeness of spirit, you openly acknowledge that there is something to be said on both sides, the woman will never then say, as would ordinarily be expected, 'Oh but there's a lot on your side too.' But thus:

MAN: (*smiling warmly*): I see your point, now, and I think there's a lot in what you say.

WOMAN: Quite so. And then there' s *another* thing. . . .

In other words women triumph by disregarding ingrained male rules of argument. Yet we have records of men who still try actually to say 'Let's sort of talk it out quietly. No need to talk *loudly,* anyhow, is there?'

No need to warn that the woman will reply:

'I never know whether, in this kind of "discussion", it's best to talk to you very firmly or very gently. Which do you prefer?'

Then again it is worth studying women with their women friends. Women are in manner much more friendly with their friends than men with theirs, and often keep men at bay by suggesting, in a sort of simultaneous flooding of the telephone, that 'here at last is someone I can talk to'. But they are expert at keeping these female acquaintances at bay, or handicapping their visits by imposing restrictions.

I am thinking of the ploys of Mrs Woking, who has lessons on bridge from Krinkelman, and lessons on dahlia gardening from Walpole Nurseries. We can take lessons from her.

(Telephone rings)
VOICE: Can I bring Ferdiepoops?
MRS WOKING: (*pausing, though she knows the voice perfectly*): Is that you, Aggie?
AGGIE: Can I bring Woopiferd?
MRS WOKING: What—your dog?
AGGIE: Ferdinand has got one of his mother-love fits on (hasn't he, Poop Woops). You've never met Woopy, have you?
MRS WOKING: I have, indeed. Look—
AGGIE: Oh—don't say your great husband isn't an animal lover.

Now comes the key line. The Dog must be warned off but owner is a reasonable fourth at bridge. So do not point out that the dog seems to be continually dissolving in a series of soft smells. Don't speak of the too long postponed euthanasia. If there can be a gleam of truth in the remark do certainly say 'My bitch is on heat'. Otherwise our choice would be for the more intricate and yet simply effective 'streaming eyes' defence.

MRS WOKING: I feel an awful fool—but No! Any dog even remotely in the Papuan poodle class makes my eyes go dark red. It's an allergy I've always had. Millions of inoculations. No use. Just talking about it makes me want to sneeze. . . .

Mrs Woking did not regard herself as a virtuoso of unfavourable physiological reactions: the method was so instinctive that she believed it was true. When a nice old dependable Goren Weak No Trump like Mrs Marion began to spoil Wednesday bridge evenings because she was soaking her neck in a scent known as Swing High, players at her table looked glazed, half-gassed. Mrs Woking was on the telephone at once:

'Look, darling, I won't tell her name. It's embarrassing. One of our number. The smell of scent brings on her knee twitch. She's been psychoe'd fifty times. Worse than ever. Knee comes right up to the chin sometimes. Has been known to knock the table over. It's an allergy. Pass the word round, will you?'

Women who are real bridge-playing women go to splendid lengths to preserve their bridge fours intact: and nothing must be allowed to break them up, and no person, with the possible exception of an only son on ten days leave from an aircraft carrier under orders to sail to the Far East. This Mrs Woking had, and he was home on this exact leave: and actually she did say to him 'Now we are specially leaving Wednesday for you to do anything you like—*anything*. I only mention Wednesday because that day the average age round the dinner table will be about 62, you poor darling!'

This got rid of the son; but Cogg-Willoughby, a regular Wednesday person and important because he had once played lawn-tennis with Terence Reese, tells me that he remembers this particular Wednesday well because Mrs Woking had recently had a letter from her best friend, Bloom, whom Cogg happened to know. She was called 'Bloom' because Bloomington was her surname and at the Essler School of Orthopaedic Nursing, where they met, shortened forms of surnames were the rule. Mrs Woking liked Bloom, if only to talk about old times and find out what had happened to 'Mac' and 'Park'. Whenever Bloom goes South to the Home Counties ('Come any time', says

Mrs Woking) she turns up. This time Bloom suggested herself for the Wednesday the 17th.

This coincided with the bridge evening: and there was a very strong danger that Bloom would want to play. Mrs Woking was not a snob but Bloom's strange Cumberland accent would be a distraction. Moreover it was certain that Bloom, because it was a party, would, in order as she would think to counteract her rather homely looks, lean strongly on her character of Good Sort. In addition, she would be 'wearing her niftiest dress for your party.' But what was really serious was that Bloom would be persuaded to play in the third rubber and would for the ninetieth time need the Blackwood convention explained to her, by difficult mathematical equation. Bloom has to be ditched: and it must be done without a particle of offence. This was Mrs Woking's letter:

'Bloomer Pie—Yes, do come—and help us in our minor crisis here. I have promised to give over our house, on that Wed. evening to a bun fight in aid of our Protection Society. The Borough Council are trying to pull down our few remaining Victorian houses. We have to stand by as members of the Committee. Let me fix you with Aunt Edith for that night'. . . .

Examples of Male Detachments

Men can learn from women this first step in detachment—this nipping in the bud of a disagreeable characteristic of the friend.

If there is one talent which the writer, for instance, would like to eradicate from his female friends, it is the ability to write. If the professional author has one certain natural enemy, it is the successful authoress. There are many proved exceptions to this rule, like the Brownings, though one can wonder if even Robert Browning was one thousand per cent contented with his rôle as the W. H. of Elizabeth Barrett's love sonnets. But how can the author keep at bay, for instance, the woman writer who has had wide popular sales among young middle-aged people and who has also had great success on television with her spiritual expression and her humane attitude to human problems?

When she visits your house, accept her, if she is of good appearance, warmly. Then after a time persuade her 'to come through to the back part' of the house 'Because it would thrill our nanny . . . perhaps you might say one word to her.' Or say 'She particularly likes the serious bit of your book at the end, where you suggest what religion really means . . . you are kind . . . remember, she's a shade deaf.'

It is the women of fine appearance who must most industriously be kept in their place, or the familiar state of wooing through weakness, i.e., falling in love in order to fill up a gap in the conversation, will supervene.

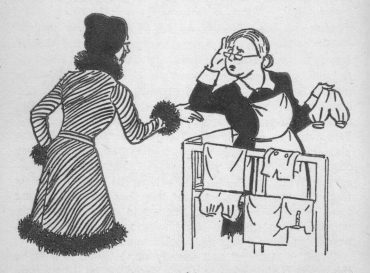

Ingenuity of Monty Ray

The man should assume a positive attitude. Our champion anti-woo lifemen shine in the more difficult situations. Take Monty Ray, the ex TV actor, who specialized in one-up cars with a dummy '5.2' embossed on the back. If he wanted to take his new old-car not to modish Garoupe but to some cheap and unheard of sea hotel near Marseilles where the roads were still reasonably empty, he would suddenly say to Phyllis:

'Poor old Eden Rock.'

'What's wrong?' Phyllis might answer.

'They're losing a thousand dollars a day, according to Jerry Corbett, who's just come back. Glorious sunshine beating down on empty sand in the Garoupe Bay. The drift's begun with a vengeance.'

'What drift?'

'To La Pire de Saint Christophe.'

Phyllis would go off quite happily to La Pire de Saint Christophe.

Monty was equally resourceful in his capacity as producer of that excellent little acting company, the Horton Bay Buskins. He was successful not because he knew anything about the theatre but because of his immaculate lifemanship, without a piece of which no stage director can conduct more than two rehearsal calls and still keep the respect even of the call boy. Mrs X ('Mrs Pat,' we called her) was not only seriously inclined to woo Monty, she also always played the lead in the Winter Play. She was competent and, more important, her husband was Manager of Willis and Monk, and ran up the costumes for us free. But the leading part for this year involved a long scene of tragic sorrow, and this would unleash Mrs Pat's well-known powers of stage weeping, and her snuffles would somehow damp the whole evening.

'Well,' ('Mrs Pat' had already said) 'What is it to be this year? If I'm going to be murdered, do let it be a little later than Act II. You remember last year—'

But Monty had already decided either to do this drama 'period,' and play it for laughs, or to give the main part to Phyllis, and he was obviously going to give the main part to Phyllis. How to banish Mrs Pat? Monty rose to the occasion. Mrs Pat discovered him frowning over the book.

'Surely there is better early Lonsdale than this?' Monty seemed to be saying half to himself. 'Read the play and tell me what you think. There is the big part of course— but (for God's sake don't tell anybody I told you this) *read carefully* the *much smaller* part of the dotty caretaker as well. Pat . . . do you want to steal the play?'*

* I would like to mention here the work of our best-known 'quick gambit' anti-wooman, Timothy Pikkins. He specialized in the five minute parley. When Wick, (the P.A.S. star of p. 41) became No 2 in Fisheries, and momentarily queen expert on the herring glut, it made her feel more than ever that she had an equal grasp of such subjects as Lines of Communication in the Eighth Army or the merits of Franco. Perkins said that he had lived fairly near the Franco circle himself (his beach holiday at Marbella, 160 miles away), and that he personally found that Wick's kind of confident half knowledge 'cast doubt on her equally dogmatic, if presumably better founded, statements on Too Much Fish'.

To the implacable foreign woman, who (p. 27) looked at Englishmen with a glance which suggested they were all Boy Scouts, Timmy would talk slowly in ultra Churchillian French about some place which sounds romantic if you haven't actually been there, like Tangier or Las Vegas. Or he would say in English 'Ah, you come I believe from the Province which gave birth to the Chevalier Leon de Percevaux'. This would actually produce an uneasy smile, from the foreigner.

Attacking the Primal Problem

Superficial beauty . . .

But we have been dealing with details long enough. The overall problem, for men, constantly recurs—the undermining influence of Female Beauty.

How to keep beauty one-down—put beauty in its place? Women are at their most deft when a good looking rival needs counterblasting. They can say smilingly 'you're looking different' or 'You've done something to your hair, haven't you?' with an intonation which suggests their rival is about to cross the borders of Shangri-la and that a thousand cracks are already appearing in the edifice of her 'amazing youthfulness.'

Yet the truly youthful beauty, the girl of perfect features and exactly charming figure, has an iron grip on life, and can rule the roost. She regards herself as by right the control, the centre, of the party. Yet the young man of courage must counter. Can she be even slightly dented? We must not give up without a struggle. If for instance she has the untouched and untouchable look of a Botticelli or Lippi nun model then talk of how charm, as dis-

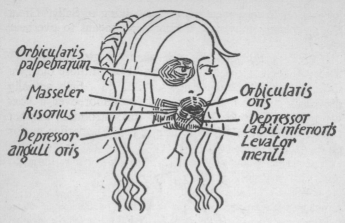

. . . showing underdevelopment of superficial facial muscles.

tinct from classical beauty, depends on the mobility of the features. Generalize about 'the 'luckiest girl in the world being the one the *superficial muscles* of whose face are highly developed, so that her most transient thoughts are mirrored on her countenance.'

Suitable territory for Sally to be distantly glimpsed running across.

'Yes, she's very sweet, if you're talking of Sally,' Great Young Beauty may say, having been meant to overhear this.

'Sally?' (picking up this cue, whatever girl you meant) 'Did you see her run across the paddock in those old gym shoes of hers? Of course, she's a child. . . .' Sally actually did have beautiful colouring and was moreover a year younger than Great Beauty, and this introduces another element which the deft practitioner could underline at this point—the absolute naturalness of every girl in the party except Great Beauty, who has more important things to think about, namely, great beauty.

Vikki was typical. Her almost sickening prettiness so often induced in men a mood of hang-dog and adoring gloom. How one grew to hate the long escalator up to the exit from Hampstead tube station, how one dawdled over the longish little walk to her flat, in 2a Willow Road. She was something to be got rid of *in toto*. A simple turn on the heel was all that was required: but how prettily the telephone would ring five days later, to the hour.

'Oh—hallo' she would say. One would immediately visualize long lashes trembling, lips with the little sad look. A baby, really: and fatuously one would cheer up tremendously even though one felt certain, as soon as one put the telephone down, that even while she was speaking to you, some ghastly man in a flowered shirt had just driven up outside her flat in an American car the size of an aircraft carrier, which Vikki would think wonderful.

My own original Vikki was long, long pre-war: and mention of her makes me think of poor Freddie, who took a Third in English Literature at Oxford when everybody expected him to get a first. The reason was Vikki. And the fact that she knew not a single line of Byron, to say nothing of Yeats and Rupert Brooke (Freddie's three favourite love poets at this time) somehow increased his slavery to her. He unloosed his literary-historical thoughts on this to me and would compare himself to Odysseus bewitched by Circe; or, when he was in the University Cadet

Unit, to the Duke of Wellington pursuing Harriet Wilson and shouting outside her front door when she was in bed with Argyll, or whoever it was.

'You must leave her', I said, when he purposely failed to get his job as assistant Literary Lecturer at Tokio.

Original picture of Vikki.

'But how?' he said.

Ah yes, how. Send her a beautifully packed orchid with the final note? Dispatch a witty letter, the result of 5 drafts and a morning's walking up and down on Primrose Hill? She will take no notice whatever. 'The problem is to get rid of your own Vikkiness,' I said. 'Think of it as taking medicine, making a parachute jump, seeing *The*

Ring from the back of the old gallery if you don't like Wagner.' A friend can be very helpful here, and I was trying. My rule with him was not to say 'It's nothing.' 'You'll have forgotten her next week.' 'It's incredible that you should even glance at that little clot. When are you going to start calling her names?' No. I kept saying:

'The pain is intense. You are doing well. Stick at it. Call me tomorrow. Have breakfast before you decide to refuse that tutorship in Durban.'

I didn't say 'just leave her' because I knew that Vikki would write to Freddie in about six weeks and say he was 'being funny' and that the sight of her huge handwriting, like the mark of an extravert leopard, would pull him back to slavery again. In the end I persuaded him to write a dignified note:

'I want to retain the picture of you which, in my mind's eye, I will carry about for ever.'

Did she get that letter? Did she drop it on the floor when she got to 'mind's eye?'

As a matter of fact she didn't: and there is, of course, the usual sort of sequel to this story.

I happened to be with Vikki when she got Freddie's 'dismissal' note.

'I want to retain the picture . . .' Vikki read out the sentence. 'He's getting at me,' she said. 'Oh dear.'

'Yes' I said.

'At last he's seen me as a cold-hard-bitch.' She said these three words as if they were one. 'Of course I am. Because certain men, and your friend Freddie is one of them, bring out the cold-hard-bitch in me to the Nth.'

'They have my sympathies.'

'You don't understand.'

I smiled. 'Poor Freddie.'

'*Nonsense.* It's their fault. They say meet me at eight and they are there every time at ten minutes to. They say they will ring at six, and they *ring at six*. It sends me raving mad. While Johnny . . . oh he's a fool . . . says he'll ring "on Wednesday" and I stay in all day Wednesday,

I daren't even go to the lavatory on Wednesday, I daren't turn the bath taps on in case I don't hear the telephone bell. . . .'

'And what happens?'

'He doesn't ring.'

I looked sympathetic.

'But I shall miss Freddie terribly. I do realise that he is a much better man than Johnny, or even than Jingo. It would be awful if he really left me. Do you think he means it? I think I'll just give him a ring.'

'Don't,' I said, putting my hand on her arm for a moment. And that, of course, was the beginning of the long painful story of me and Vikki.

Limp Management

I recall a curious instance of the diplomatic get-out, a way of avoiding *the results* of an objectionably female woo trait.

In essence, it is a device brought into play through the possession of a handicap. It is often very useful in the man v. woman situation, if the man has something wrong with him. He may, for example, simply walk with a thick stick, and as this is a technique I use myself, perhaps for once I may write here in the first person. I do in fact have a slight limp, the result of an old peace wound—a fall in a picture gallery.*

I discovered that so long as the slight limp was preserved, and even without it, the stick gave me something. It added weight to my personality. It was a perfect excuse not to take part in a mixed foursome at golf, if I didn't fancy my opponents—if, for instance, the opposition man turned out to be a member of the Oxford and Cambridge Society, who would therefore certainly outdrive me by eighty yards minimum. A policeman hanging over your

* Insurance rates for this particular injury are, according to the celebrated actor R. R., not more than three shillings in a thousand pounds.

wrongly parked car may actually apologize if, in addition to the stick, your right knee is practically touching the ground from some apparently congenital malformation. My friend Floorman, who was perfectly prepared to use two sticks if necessary, would, when he saw a police car waiting, get his two companions to take his elbows so firmly that his feet were off the ground, while a sergeant fussed around opening doors. I have myself performed minor feats such as parking my car outside the Festival Hall for an important concert, and driving it straight into a sort of pen marked 'Conductors Only', and then half

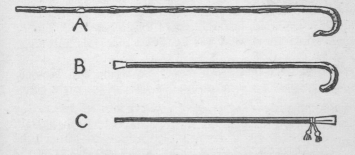

A. Crummock (Gael. cromag). Injury due to stalking.
B. War wound.
C. Injury due to trying to execute the 'bridge jump' in de Falla's Three-Cornered Hat.

crawling out of the car, bent too low almost for the stick to be much help, getting helped up the steps by the commissionaires.*

But the use of the limp against women must be especially explained for this chapter: and here Floorman regarded himself as particularly successful. No need, with the stick, to give up his seat to a woman. It was he who expected them to get up for him. More important, there was a time when Floorman was emphatically younger,

* My own idea, of attaching a realistic dummy third leg, was dropped in rehearsal. A mounted police inspector complained.

and I remember being surprised to see him with his stick when he was going to take a girl out to dine and dance.

But when I realized the girl was Trina I understood. She was very pretty in a ferocious way but she never gave you frost-bite, like Vikki. She was quite a gay little girl in the secretarial pool, but in the evenings she darkly turned to thoughts of love, and it made her look as solemn as a silent-film heroine. Glumness as a backbone to sex is an anti-woo sign in itself: but it was worse than that, for almost every evening out with Trina had to end in an 'atmosphere.' Trina liked her escort to be on his toes, to say the least of it. More specifically she wanted him, whatever the situation, in some way to suggest that he was chivalrously active in her defence. Suddenly her eyes would open wide, and she would lower her head. Floorman would know what was up. Some man was 'insulting' her.

'Do you see that awful man?' she would say. No-one could possibly see him, in the dim light of the night club.

The 'eyes like gimlets' ploy.

'Those awful eyes, staring at me. They seem to be boring through my chest. It makes me feel as if I were naked.'

Trina often was in fact unusually naked, in the evening. Adorable, but not within a thousand miles of making me, still less Floorman, want to get up and start something beginning 'Look here Sir.' I myself tried some pointedly admonitory remarks like 'the girl who is fortunate enough to possess a sophistication comparable with her beauty somehow manages to insulate herself from the possibility of unwelcome attentions.' But while congratulating myself on this phrase I had to admit that Trina hadn't taken in a word of it.

'It's horrible . . . that man's expression . . .'

But Floorman wasn't going to have any of that sort of thing. At the first sign of an Eyes Like Gimlets situation blowing up, he would smother an involuntary groan, and start feeling his leg. 'I'm sorry. Shan't be much good on the dance floor tonight,' Floorman would say.

'What's the matter, darling?'

'Look, it's swollen up to double the size—it must have touched the table leg or something.'

This usually diverted Trina, even if it were only to say 'how unpleasant for you.' To have a stick, coupled with an old rugger knee, or, better still, a War bullet which can't be extracted because of the danger of severing the saphenous nerve, so that at rare moments one is barely able to move, is a fine way of getting rid of the chivalrous protection situation.

Floorman was pretty sound when it came to deflating a woo impulse. And I remember that he always said that though the pretty ones, the beauties, were hard to handle, the most difficult of all were the calm ones. The self-sufficient ones. People like Garda—or like Asra, who was such a perfectionist of the et ceteras—never drinking or smoking all over the place, never crying over spilt milk, never taking any notice if a friend showed signs of cooling. I envied Asra her ability never to fuss or fluster. Floorman envied her poise. But it was Floorman, in the end, who asked her the question which was screaming inside all of us.

'What,' he said, 'are you poised *for*?'

5

The Coad Scale of
Progressive Rifts

Odoreida, beyond the battle in the realm of love,
yet still on occasion holding in his stomach muscles.

Students who have reached this point sometimes disappoint
us: but we feel and hope that by now they should be
what we call 'love-free.' And how they will be enjoying
the situation. There is the sense of ease, of relaxation. The
sky is larger, the wind fresher. There is the return to
friends; the glance of silent congratulation as one sidles
into the bar. There is the return to loneliness and self-
respect. Singleness is so pleasant, invigorating. No dead
weight on the pillion to slow you up on a gradient. Or
it is your open two seater you can enjoy, even if your left

hand* does occasionally search absent-mindedly for another hand to hold. No need now not to have the hood down, even in November. No dash, with harrowed brow, for the post with a letter which has been held up because of the near impossibility of thinking of something new to say daily. No treadmill walk to an obscure telephone box to make an unnecessary call demanded by the mere fact of the other person being 280 miles distant. No need to do anything, except put your feet up.†

A Simplified Test

But it is our wish to encourage, as well as to warn. And there are many today who regard themselves as being under the spell of love who yet are very much less entangled than they believe. We have been perfecting, over a period of months, a scientific series of tests, by means of which various degrees of not being in love have been graded. Old Lifemen will be glad to hear that this operation has been under the personal supervision of G. Coad-Sanderson, F.Z.S., our graph adviser under three separate managements.**

The method is known as the Coad Scale, and its basis is a simple system of visits. These surprise calls are carried out by expert questioners and quiz men. Most of these, by the way, are women: and in some areas, in their quite becoming uniformettes, and large brimmed hats inclined at a chic angle, they are becoming a familiar landmark.

Extreme cases do not interest us. It is generally accepted that couples who shout at each other at the top of their voices all day and all night can never under any circumstances be persuaded to separate. Nor can quarrels of the

* In U. S., right.
† A warning here. Some are so overwhelmed by the new sense of power that they fall in love with somebody else the very next Saturday night, out of sheer light-heartedness.
** It is the expectation of all that he will shortly be made a life peer, in which case we understand he will wish to be called Lord Sanderson of Scale.

newly engaged be taken reliably as signs for the future. The man, in particular, is so thunderstruck by the princeliness of the gesture he is making in choosing the woman that he feels this demands constant recognition. Again, fear of the life sentence exaggerates the importance even of a slight difference of taste in biscuits. 'Lovers' quarrels,' says Coad, in his introductory lecture, 'are sensible because they are exploratory; they are exaggerated on purpose. The test pilot subjects the aircraft to strains it will never meet in routine service'—a remark which is often applauded.

'What is your Coad-Sanderson?'

Our tests are confined to a relationship which is well under way, and for convenience each degree of anti-woo is marked with a number representing the percentage equivalent of the current state of non-woo of the two parties concerned.*

As an introduction to this subject we reproduce here extracts of our Coad Scale for Men, with index percentages in the margin.

Still Solid

C–S 0·5   These early categories only show, of course, evidence too slight to be denominated as even a minor rift. 0·5 is the percentage number when, instead of answering, the man smiles affectionately at girl's remarks because, though it isn't in the least her fault, she hasn't quite got the gist of the general discussion.

* There has been some resistance to our panel of questioners in certain quarters: but we on our side have kept our temper. In the mixed section of our organization, 'What is your Coad-Sanderson' is quite a regular question.

C–S 2·0 Is the grade for the man, who, when explaining things, uses a very nice voice which is at the same time a little slower or clearer than normal.

C–S 3·0 When man notices at Christmas time, that her excitement at his present is a shade absent-minded, and does not do justice to the trouble he took in choosing it for her.

C–S 3·2 When the present he chooses for her is partly rather educative, that is to say it is about a subject in which he is rather more interested than she—say, Peterson's *Wild Birds of Europe*: or *The Story of the Heavens*.

C–S 3·5 When he notices that she is unexpectedly impatient with her sister, say, or even her sister's daughter, and he makes a point of saying to himself 'Ah but think of the warm floods of affection of which she is capable.'

First Suspicion of Crack

C–S 4·0 There is something about her dress, her gestures, or the angle of her neck. Instead of reminding him of some wonderful intensification of her beauty which this detail revealed when he first got to know her, it irritatingly forces him to recollect a smothered criticism of his own or even somebody else's, like your friend Carol's. 'She's a little bit stained glass, isn't she?' which he at that time, and still does, put down entirely to jealousy.

C–S 8·0 When with absolute ease and a broad feeling of mutually affectionate friendship and respect, both agree to differ on liking football, or Dickens, or completely modern chairs, or jokes about the convention of opera, and both agree not to talk much more about these subjects.

C–S 12·0 Suddenly your face, set so long in an expression of happy love when you look at her, feels a little stiff and fixed. (This is indexed, with us, as 'smiler's cramp').

Hairline Fracture

C–S 14:0 The man is possibly beginning to be out of love when he says to himself more than once in one week 'I would be mad to grumble— me, the luckiest man in the world.'

C–S 14·5 For months Norman has been aware in a friendly way of Maurice Minniter, an old friend

of Norman's wife before they were married.
Maurice has irritated Norman, but only, really, because of the reiteration of the same
joke. Norman has been for a long time working
at his French conversation; Maurice possesses
an easy command of this language which should
not in fact surely count as a merit because he
(Maurice) was practically bi-lingual from birth
and therefore a semi-foreigner anyhow. But if
Norman uses the most ordinary French phrase,
like 'hors de combat' or even 'hors d'oeuvre' or
the place-name 'Boulogne,' Maurice always
makes a point of pretending not to understand or saying 'Well done, Normy,' sometimes adding:

'Mais tu es Parisien?'

'Well done Maurice' says Norman. 'If you
repeat a joke fifty times it's bound to be a
success.'

But Norman likes Maurice. Rivalry, he used
to say, is like *sauce piquante* (well done, Norman) to a love affair like mine with Jill. But
one day Norman found he didn't like Maurice
so much, and for a strange reason. Maurice
hadn't said a word to Jill, when they met at
the theatre bar: on the contrary he was talking
hard to a girl child nicknamed 'Hemingway',
whose hair was piled on top of her head to
the ceiling. She seemed to have one of those no-
make-up make-ups.

'Maurice is in splendid form,' Norman
couldn't help saying to Jill, as they sidled up
behind him.

'Well done, Maurice,' Norman said, as the
crowd pushed them in his direction. But what
surprised Norman, at that date, was that he
was measurably more annoyed that Maurice
was talking to Hemingway, than he would
have been if he had been talking to Jill.

Cleft

C–S 17·0 'What fantastic tricks light can play.' Suddenly, because he catches sight of her in a mirror, or because he imagines her somewhere else, he doesn't quite recognize her. Something curious about the nose, a slight downward curve —a shadow below the eye, too. She is a little older than he thought, a worried face he never usually sees, introspective, gloomily oblivious of her surroundings, like a christmas shopper in Oxford Street. Something has gone wrong. No! There she is again; the key fits, the old love-view has swum back into focus. For a moment he had thought she was someone else, and therefore someone he wasn't in love with.

C–S 21·0 She comes unexpectedly into the study where he is working and he smiles welcomingly; but at the same time, because she has left the door open he spreads his arms firmly over the desk in case any paper flutters out of position. His right hand is on the pile of letters, his left elbow firmly on the scattered flimsies of a manuscript. He waits pleasantly to see what she wants.

C–S 22·5 It is possible to be irritated not unreasonably, surely, by the fact that in spite of her contact with your not totally imperceptive eye for colour, etc., she still decorates her room in a style which must jar them both.

Fissure

C–S 23·0 He has long wondered, now he is sure. He would rather not be present when she is with her best female friend.

C–S 28·0 Her scent is delicious, so are her bath salts. But so, my God, is the smell of bracken in the sun, or a cigar-smoky billiards room, of the first touch of frost in October.

C–S 34·0 Suddenly there was something, my God, he really disapproved of. Who was that, with the angry level voice, talking too loudly? Listen.

'Can't I trust you even to put the right things in the washing basket?'

Was that really her voice?

'Look, the list is here. *In front of you.*'

Surely one doesn't talk to anybody like that. Especially a servant. It's as if she wasn't . . . oh well. No doubt it was justified. That woman can be maddeningly stupid. Why should he not be on her side?—he *must* be on her side.

C–S 35·3 Sometimes you cannot help wondering, when she says she has had an appallingly busy day, if she realizes the totally different scale, amounting to a new conception of the world of work, of your own business, such a lot of the most essential parts of which are done—how could she realize this?—when you are walking up and down the room, or taking the dog for a walk, or even reading the newspaper, or watching ('stuck in your chair,' she said) some foolish television programme.

C–S 38·0 When she says, rather teasingly, 'I can get you at the Club, no doubt', and the man thinks it might be fun (thank God he has got his lovely home attachment now) to calculate how much more time—certainly threefold—he spent at these placcs before he knew her. And this has to be set against the acquisition of a beautiful woman and wonderful companion, and this is what he chose to do.

This little group of his friends,—Walter, Fulford, B.J.,—who looked on him as the focal point of their small social gatherings must go somewhere else, that is all, and stop glancing at him as if he were a lost being, a soul under a ban. If, in fact, they have not forgotten him altogether.

C–S 39·0 He remembers the first time hc took her to *Peter Grimes*. His choice—and he took her through some of the themes beforehand, played the notes of the Passacaglia, repeating its version of the phrase '*Grimes* . . . is at his exercise.' But this time she was not attending so much—she was so tangled up, mentally, with the news of her sister's engagement. So his mind went back to the first time, when she not only took his hand in hers but—and this is the miraculous fact typical of tales told by returning travellers and never believed—but that first time she took his hand in both of hers. Both of hers. So that his stubby fist was bound round with fingers. He is back at that first seeing of Peter Grimes. He's not at this performance at all.

C–S 43·5   Leaving her—Going off on a long train journey, a lecture trip to Aberdeen, he has the feeling that 'well, I'm a temporary bachelor. A man with my own world, though,—sufficient to myself and at home in any place in the world.'

C–S 43·8   He idly day-dreams—if the ghastly thing happened and she did disappear—leave—desert— . . . whether there would not be a grain of self-satisfaction, in the intervals of his loneliness, at assuming the dignity of the man smitten by grief.

Water-Jump

C–S 45·0   When he decides for the second time running that it's no good showing her that letter he's just written because either *(a)* she won't see the point *(b)* she'll make an irrelevant comment *(c)* she won't be one hundred per cent listening.

C–S 51·0   Within twenty minutes of making love to her, he went back to the little argument they were having before, with almost the same touch of asperity.

C–S 52·0   He decides to make no comment whatever on her new hair style.

C–S 54:0 He thinks it's a pity she seemed to have had two large martinis before she joined the party, but after some hesitation he's not going to say anything about it.

C–S 59:0 He is certain that it is indicated that he should not be present when Claudia—still 'his' Claudia in the eyes of the world surely—is meeting Angela or Lydia: and he is equally certain that at the beginning of the meal with this girl, Claudia will look mysterious and reserved, and before it is halfway through will be talking full pelt about her difficulties and it will obviously be her difficulties with him.

C–S 61·0 The time has come when surely to hop round (she seems to have forgotten altogether the small fact that in 1942 half your right big toe was practically shot clean off in the Desert)— to limp to open the door for her every time she pauses slightly as if expecting it, seems absurd. . . . Surely it will seem unnecessarily fussy even to her. People are smiling already.

Crevasse

C–S 64·0 When you start in private practising things you are going to say to her, just as you did when you were falling in love with her. Now with a heavy difference.

C–S 64·5 When the gist of such remarks is instructional, and delivered in a kind of public relations tone of voice, which you hear echoing in your head for hours afterwards.

C–S 67:0 He really wants to beat her at lawn tennis, and send her short ones, because she's as lazy as hell and running won't do her any harm. And when he serves his hardest, he almost half wishes the ball would hit her on the knee. Sometimes, he says out loud, but not so that she can hear, things like 'Bang'.—'Swipe'—'Smash'.*

Canyon

C–S 67·8 When you feel that what she did then—telling B.K. about your mistake—was something mechanically hard, if not mean—something outside your own nature—that is why you never noticed that tendency in her before.

C–S 74·0 Losing any desire to show that you are a 'happy couple'—taking her hand, having intent conversation as if you hadn't seen her for days. And if you look towards her at a dinner party it is a parody of the proud, warm glance you once gave her.

C–S 78·0 You finally stop insisting that she is somewhere in the picture when you take a photograph, or even wanting her to be in it.

* But beware, here, if your service is never a very strong one. She may, as Phyllis did against Monty, send them back harder than they came.

C–S 75·0 You are glad she is going out without you,
though irritated at her manner of doing it, and
it will bring on the depression.

When we first saw this list of Coad-Sanderson's, we con-
gratulated him on its scientific integrity. Only Cogg-Willoughby demurred.

COGG: There is, if one may say so, a certain 'lack of
heart.'

GATTLING-FENN: Heart? They don't want heart, they
want a life belt. They're stuck in a life jam.

COGG: *(slowly wiping his spectacles)*: When the tide is
full out, both of them, the man and the woman, are
stranded. They sit high and dry, at a slightly unnatural
tilt; with all the imperfections of their hulls in full
view of each other, deprived of the element which
brought them jointly to life. For the time being, they
are unable to move.

GATTLING: Personally I would like to change that meta-
phor.

FOUNDER: Fine.

GATTLING: I would say they'd run out of petrol.

FOUNDER: That's good, too; but the other one's better.

GATTLING: No reserve tanks to keep them going.

COGGS: Ah, yes *(putting his hand on Gattling's arm)*.

GATTLING: *(withdrawing arm)*: Ah *what?*

COGG: First reserve tank of affection.

FOUNDER: Yes?

COGG: Second reserve tank of friendship.

FOUNDER: Good, good. So what do they do?

GATTLING: Part, if they can.

FOUNDER: Not too easy, if you're stranded.

COGG: More—far more—difficult than falling in love.

FOUNDER: It calls, surely for another chapter.

GATTLING: Calls for another.

6

Basic Disentanglement Techniques

Evil Results of Spurning

If Lifemanship can be of assistance anywhere in a crisis of woo, it can help with the woo exit. Clumsy detachment is clumsy lifemanship; and spurning, at Yeovil, is tabu.

Not only is it unsporting: there is also the question of the social stigma. Yet there are two exceptions to this rule. Spurning is O.K. (i) if the spurner is ugly and the spurnee is handsome. Nobody would have blamed Barbara Allen, in the ballad, if she had had a perpetually red nose, snuffles, and protruding upper teeth. It would have put a different light on the desire of the young man to turn his face to the wall.

Secondly it may be said in the most general possible terms that it is more O.K. for women to spurn than it is for men. If the falling out of love is one sided, the detachment should in any circumstances be as careful as the removal of a leech. But if it is man leaving woman, precautions must be doubled. Whatever the state of his own conscience, her relatives, his notions of chivalry—all weigh in against him like an army of elephants. If the woman seeks revenge, she will be universally applauded.

Her action will be justified by ancient myth. Medea, after she had fallen in love with Jason, was almost too solicitous in her wifely support. She not only made it possible for Jason to perform certain apparently impossible tasks, such as sowing dragons' teeth; she also murdered her young brother in order to delay her avenging father. She went further. To circumvent anti-Jasonite activities, Medea fixed the boiling alive of Pelias. Therefore when Jason spurned Medea and left her to marry the daughter of Creon, it was mythologically correct play for Medea to kill the bride, kill the bride's father, and, because Jason begot them, kill her own children.*

Basic Male Method: The Importance af Being Noble

It is not our purpose, here, to discuss basic disentanglement techniques for women. The subject is too complex for a

* I myself had a rather similar experience when I was Literary lecturer to the East Penge Tutorial Class of the Workers' Education Association in 1929. I was grateful to my class secretary for her help, but could not bring myself to share her interest in spiritualism. She reported me unfavourably to the Assistant Director of Studies, in Pimlico.

first text book, the scales too weighted in the woman's favour. It is well known that women are able to keep spurned males in attendance for years by turning them into faithful sympathizers, or sound old, trustworthy, Major Dobbins who spend their lives never mentioning the name of a woman in the mess.

For men, the first rule undoubtedly is to adopt the Gentlemanly-noble. It has been the accepted method in modern times in England since the best pre-Ibsen early Pinero kind of drama. At the end of Act II the guest finds that the wife has taken a fancy to him. In 1882 this has to be put the other way round—he has taken a fancy to the wife. In the play his heart is broken, but he remains calm. At the end of Act III he has packed before breakfast. He is ready to go.

The Farewell, 1885.

BUTLER: Excuse me, sir. Perkins is outside sir. Shall I put in your trunk?

HILARY FORSYTH: Thank you Jarvis *(he has not turned but is still staring up the staircase with a look on his face which we shall never forget)*.

Thank you. Bring me my hat and coat.

BUTLER: I have it here sir.

HILARY *(aside)*: Do not rouse her ladyship now, Jarvis. On no account rouse her. But—give her this note.

However old-fashioned it may seem, this can still be the basic way. *Provided the writer of the note believes in the character he is assuming.*

Specimen Letters

'Forgive me, yes, I am going,' is what he has written, and continues delicately to indicte that 'Plato is a fraud.' (i.e., that his love can be no longer Platonic.) If the woman was unmarried, the noble withdrawal had to be more distant. Thus (correct for 1878):

'I shall fully anticipate an answer to this by Wednesday's post. If a letter does not arrive by that time, I shall accept Mrs Lafont's invitation to go with her and her daughters to the continent, as I presume my presence at your father's house for shooting this season would be considered *de trop*'.

Direct nobility of this kind can no longer be expressed if only because we no longer have the language. But it is still possible to be nobly-unworthy. Sentences may be taken from the following:

'No, I can't come. I'd like to see you all again so enormously that I'm afraid of saying how much. But I can't, and I'm not going to indulge in a great orgy of self-pity on that account. I've had another of my "bad" months. You remember my celebrated Report

on Waterways that you hated and hated me for because I worked on it all through half of every night
that week? Well, I showed it to Forester and he sat on
it for 10 days and then had me up to tell me that if I'd
taken the trouble to study the old company records I'd
have seen that this was the same plan, in almost the pre-
cise words, of the proposal adopted in 1954, and successful in that year because of the Soft Steel Subsidy. So I've
got to start all over again: and my great plan of stopping
cigs. will have to be put off once more, and another holiday will be impossible. I don't *drink,* as you know—
never have—but I believe I am discovering what it is to
be a tippler. I just pour a little Haig into a tooth glass,
every now and then. . . .'

Or it is possible to suggest that to part can be the most
satisfying kind of meeting:

'The point is that this is a sort of beginning, more
exciting, in a way, than anything we've known already.
To say that we're "going to part" is a Jesuitical jug-
gling with words. Don't you get this feeling too—I know
you do—that we're almost more closely in touch the
further we are, topographically, apart? I seem to be
exchanging ideas with you, comparing notes, asking
your advice and criticism without speaking—and sometimes even indeed without writing. . . .'

One can even, if the letter is rightly worded, take the
initiative in saying 'we must part.' But only if, as in the
case of Jack Crowfoot, the man is driven half mad by
the girl Susan's endless demands for petty attention.
I saw Joe, and I saw he was suffering from door-opener's
shuffle and constantly-rising-to-his-feet knee. I advised him
to write as follows (adding a few spelling mistakes):

'We must part, We have to make a clean and absolute break—I mean there must be a mental gap be-

tween us the size of Crystal Palace, besides the physical one. I want you to realize that every day I shall be writing you a long letter, in spirit if not in actual fact.

Wrong. Comic drawing inappropriately inserted by Gattling-Fenn in his goodbye letter.

'You ask me if I read your last letter because I "haven't answered your question on the last page." *That* is simply because your handwriting reached explosion point just there; I couldn't read a word of it. I have never known anybody draw their own portrait so vividly simply by calligraphy. I would not wish you in any way different. I shall miss those bombshell envelopes on my doormat because I know that now you are going to write less often and make up for that on our glorious private intercom of thought waves'.

If you Can't be Noble, Attack

Unfortunately Sue smelt a rat, because she knew that Joe would never know how to use a semi-colon. But the letter was right in spirit because there was *no hint of apology*.

The great DON'T in this situation is 'Never Say Sorry'. 'This is a terrible letter to have to write.' Never write it.

'Nothing you can say about me could be too bad, too bitter. . . .' Never write that either.

'I have crossed out these words fifteen times . . . you will think me an unspeakable cad . . . it would be better for you if I had never been born.'

Get that tone of voice right out of your mind. Better than apology is accusation.

'You have made our friendship impossible. Do you realize the breaking strain under which I have been living these last few months?'

She may not understand what you are talking about, but she will not feel stranded. She will even be able to regard herself as a weaver of destinies, or at least as a participator in disaster.

If you feel you are letting her off too lightly, list the faults of the woman *as if they were your own*. This was a Coad-Sanderson method.

'I felt so surely last time, when we had that rather idiotic row about theatre tickets—I hadn't realized, even fractionally, that you didn't really want to see the Old Vic full length Hamlet. I was so busy preening myself on having got the tickets—through Bill Mather. Anyhow, suddenly I heard myself developing a sort of *plaintive cadence*—and I simply dared not risk meeting you again until I had worked it out of my system: if I am going to get *silently pained*, I know I must get away for a little personal therapy. Any relationship which includes *regular lapses into coldness* is intolerable. "Never be offended: never, never have a hurt voice" —Ah, the old, vital rule.'

Coad was particularly conscious, when he wrote this letter, that this woman, after 18 months of entertainment out which had cost him he reckoned something in the nature of £765, never said thanks even for the opening of Coventry Cathedral or a seat in the same row as Princess Margaret for the première of *Victors,* a film which he had not particularly wanted to see. But he also knew that though he had even gone to the extent of hiring a chauffeur-driven car (so that her feet wouldn't have to tread even on ten yards of uncarpeted pavement), and that though she had been the first to criticize the smallest lapse in these arrangements, this girl would never think for one moment that she herself was being even faintly got at, still less that Coad was rather brilliantly striking back.

But the lifeman is never not quite a gentleman. He never wounds pride—this must be the first rule of successful gentle detachment. Observe also the effectiveness of the *shatteringly brief hint of personal disaster* note.

It's no good. I've tried every way and I'm out. I'm boarding up the entrance, locking myself in, in some kind of real sense. I have discovered the meaning of the word excommunication.

The girl can—will certainly—show this letter to her woman friend. 'I'm so worried about Dick. He wrote me such a strange letter.'

This wording is very close to the text used by Jeremy B. when he was extricating himself from the red-haired girl Dorothy Jackson-Blake, who was in advertising, Berkeley Square. It did not work because the very next morning Dorothy J-B saw Jeremy driving a Miss Gunnery down Davies Street in a scarlet open sports car.

Study the finesse of painless leaving. A civilized performer can without apologizing use the word 'apology' in such a way that the girl feels that it is she who should be asking pardon. The writer of the following must believe in his letter: indeed it may not undesirably contain a touch of truth. 'I', the man is saying* 'am a man who loves

* Copyright Lifemanship Publication Corp.

too much. I am in danger of losing my self-respect.' (Ideally this letter should be written in Chancery Italic script, well to the right of the page).

> *I don't know what to call this letter—an apology for loving, perhaps, certainly not an apology for leaving. You must have had an extraordinary sense of release, of relaxation, when you saw the last of me. Love which becomes an obsession has lost its cleanness, its fine definition. I shall keep away from you in order to recognize myself again and know the boundaries by which I am contained. Then perhaps if once more we can become two worlds, complete—two twin stars circling round each other, connected but separate—you will be able to enjoy me more, and I shall at any rate have regained my self-respect.**

Dangers of Compatibility

An acutely difficult detachment situation arises if the two persons involved are 'made for each other'. Yet often the need for separation is no less urgent. It is easy to separate iron and wood, but mixed whisky and soda, which go well together, need a laboratory.

Constant sympathetic understanding can destroy. Above

* Copyright Lifemanship Publication Corp.

all perpetual forgiveness turns the veins to water and destroys love. 'Oh my dear, if only I had understood' is all right at the matinée but loses its effect when it is repeated at the evening performance. After a time the woman may long to stub her toe, if only for the comfort of feeling something solid. Notice how the prospect of perpetual compatibility seems to take the fun out of a good story, a fact which clouds the final chapters of the hero and heroine part of nineteenth century novels, particularly Dickens', although the atmosphere may resemble calm before a storm.

Take, for instance, the case of Caroline Few and Harold Doe. At his home in Wembley, Harold had been spoilt. But when, after reading Butler's *Way Of All Flesh* he 'broke away', and took a bed sitter in Frognal, Hampstead, he soon regretted it, and began sneaking back to Wembley 'to see his old Mother'. Actually these visits rather irritated Mrs Doe.

Caroline Few was just the woman for Harold. She realized at once his need for being looked after. Perfect.

'Come along now!'

She had made a salad. He did not like salad but the lack of it might be the cause of his eyes watering.

'Poor pink eye,' Caroline would say. 'You must have some carrot.' He had carrot six times running.

'By the way, how on *earth* do you get cigarette ash on the small of your back?' She was always hedging him round with little tin ash trays by his side. 'I suppose you loathe getting new shoe laces?' Harold felt a twinge of claustrophobia.

Soon Caroline began to overdo it.

When he began to put on weight, she switched him to special sugarless tinned pears, completely without taste.

Harold began to feel suffocated, and to think of ways of detaching himself. Yet how? They were perfectly suited! And this was the barrier.

Harold was an apprentice psychologist at the Realfood Laboratories on the North Circular, and he prided himself on devices. He had the idea of writing a letter to Caroline *as if from his mother,* imitating her handwriting, which in fact Caroline had never seen. 'Caroline you are not considerate enough', was the keynote—reversing the facts.

> You don't realize that 'kiddy' (as we always call Harold) gets fussed and hampered if some things aren't right for him. Certain things—like having his marmalade super fresh, not out of the bottom of the jar—are absurdly important to him I know. But as you know too so well someone who is in any sense, as he is most tremendously, an artist. . . .

While she read this letter Caroline became subjected to the curious law that it is impossible to spoil anybody if somebody else is doing it more so. She began to feel 'I have no patience with that kind of person. I like a man'.

In a general healthy atmosphere of mutual disagreement, Harold found himself free again.

But how does it work if the compatibility is still closer —if it depends on an exact similarity of tastes? This, in brief, is the story of Vanessa and Carrington. Vanessa had 'good' features in a Greek way, and Carrington did not mind that they sometimes looked a little sweaty. Vanessa 'hated women who always went about with a beauty box', which meant in effect that she was very careful herself only to use make-up on certain areas which she considered 'natural'. Vanessa had written a 'Portrait of Loneliness', published by the Hogarth Press, which was really herself as a child. Carrington, who had an exactly cut beard, was a real author, a literary historian and lecturer, short sighted, hard working. He became infatuated with Vanessa's 'animal warmth', her cat-like grace and her only occasionally shiny profile (she seemed to be perpetually in profile). Most women writing to an accepted author think it advisable to use no punctuation mark more discriminatory than a dash. Not so, Vanessa. She started the correspondence like this:

'I was glad to get your letter. Your envelope lay on the hall table (I had no other correspondence) "like the lone waterthrush whose stillness pleads for company". At first I put your letter aside, for better digestion later: to tell the truth, the postman who brought it had a bad cold, and I thought that this might mean bad news ('The postman himself is hoarse . . .') However, all is well, and you will see me preening my enjoyment like my mother's tortoiseshell puss, being in general prone to a fine fit of purring.'

Some might regard this letter as a bit of a blow: but Carrington, who had been an editor of Keats, was glad to find Vanessa at home in his own subject. He sent her a letter in rather the same style, and enjoyed writing out Keats's posthumous cat sonnet, believing Vanessa would not know this too well.

When she wrote back showing her familiarity with what Robert Gittings had said about this sonnet it only

Carrington thinking 'perfect Elizabeth Siddall' when he first sees Vanessa.

partly pleased Carrington, because he had always felt hitherto that Gittings was rather muscling in on his territory. For whatever reason he didn't answer till he had had two more letters from Vanessa, in which the literariness was spread even thicker, while his chance of having a moderately animal affair with Vanessa seemed to be becoming correspondingly remote.

Soon Carrington found himself getting briefer and blunter in his own missives. This only made Vanessa redouble her literary references, and when he wrote her something too bluff altogether, starting 'how's the old quotesman' followed by something coarse from Ben Jonson, Vanessa wrote back a rather briefer letter. She said she enjoyed his sanguine humor, and had always admired the 'vivid *immediacy* of *exactly* contemporary speech.' Carrington couldn't bear it. He began to make obviously inaccurate text references, in the hope that Vanessa would 'see through him.' To Carrington's joy and with a tinge of relief on her side as well, this worked perfectly. Almost immediately Vanessa started a correspondence with a taxi driver who had had a poem accepted by *Encounter*.

OLD LITERARY LIFEMAN: Ah, the gentle art of painless detachment!

THIRTEEN YEAR OLD GIRL STUDENT: Is that all?

OLL: Well, we want to end this book on a happy note.

TYOGS: Why?

OLL: *(patting girl):* Well we all want to be happy people, don't we? Besides this is a family book.

TYOGS: *(moving away):* But nobody could be more family than I am, and I am much more interested in *painful* detachment. Millions of lovers end up by murdering each other,—or sending each other mad by slow invisible forms of torture—

OLL: Well, I know . . . yes, in a *way*. You never heard, I suppose, Cogg-Willoughby's lecture on how famous literary men got rid of their women?

TYOGS: Tell me about it.

THE COGG-WILLOUGHBY LECTURE

*Founder (with Director of Illustration on his right)
asks Cogg-Willoughby a question.*

Appendix

Some thoughts on the Principles of Anti-Woo as Observed in the Behaviour of Literary Men*

by Howard Cogg-Willoughby

'All literature is Lifemanship.'

'All literature is an escape from Lifemanship.'

Cogg-Willoughby paused such a long time after this good opening that we thought something had gone wrong. Then suddenly he started again, speaking too fast:

'How can we equate these often repeated sayings? The answer is simple. When the creative spirit flags, lifemanship takes its place. In the absence of inspiration, the writer concentrates on the appearance of inspiration. Or he may fall back on the *mannerisms* of genius. More generally he will add touches to that detailed and flattering portrait of himself which he likes his readers to remember. All this is lifemanship, and almost all writers, at one time or another, are lifemen. "Blake is the only poet without a mask."

'Lifewriter Galsworthy, who wrote 1,500,000 words without an "I", is constantly painting his own portrait, of the man who keeps himself in the background. Bernard Shaw filled in the gaps in his genius by painting his self-portrait as "G.B.S."—unquenchable, unbeatable, maniacally sane, clear-cut whatever the evidence, the unscientific "scientific attitude." G.B.S. is Shaw's lifemanship. In Coleridge the contrast is even more exaggerated—between

* This is a very much shortened version of a paper which was read by Cogg-Willoughby before an appreciative audience at the Hardington Mandeville Literary Society. The wording is his own, but the ideas in it were originally thrashed out by all of us, round a table, with mugs filled—'Rather an Elizabethan atmosphere,' said a young printer. 'The Mermaid in the great days', he added—fooling, of course.

112

Coleridge the Great and S.T.C. the Lifeman, misunderstood, unappreciated by family and public, wrongly accused, in the face of impressive plans for the future, of never doing anything.

'S.T.C. is Coleridge's lifemanship.

'Side by side with Hemingway the man is Hemingway the manly—next door to artist tender is lifeman tough. In others, often the most vulnerable, the lifemanship is narrowed into the determination never to be one down— in Pope and Dr Johnson, Wilde and Thomas Carlyle.'

There was applause when Cogg said the name 'Carlyle'. After some more havering he got onto the real subject of his discourse.

'If literary men are good lifemen, we would expect them to be particularly deft in their handling of the Falling Out of Love situation. But in fact the opposite is the truth— and indeed there are only two successful gambits in this field which are particularly associated with writers. The first is the glorification of the discarded love in immortal poetry. This is done with almost mechanical regularity, so that biographers get in the habit of saying "the year of 'To Phoebe'," or "this was the 'cruel pendant of a sceptered flower' period".'

'More useful has been the poets' tendency to keep the other sex at bay by letting it be known that the "Julia" of the early love sonnets was the only love, and that it went wrong, and that there has never really been anyone since. This One Lovemanship is perhaps the best thing that literary men have ever provided for us under the heading of love avoidance: and it has often enabled them, for the purposes of their art, to look at the opposite sex with iron detachment.

'There is some evidence that Jane Austen was a One Love expert: there is certain evidence of her detachment. Her description of wrong wooing methods, by the Reverend Collins, of Elizabeth, is of technical use under more than one heading of Anti-Woo. Collins wooed by numbers and the method was wrong because (1) it was devoid of spontaneity and undertaken with (2) a trace of condescension, known as (3) "paying attentions". At the Ball where this happened he was so (4) thick-skinned that he did not realize that he was unwelcome or that (5) he was preventing Elizabeth, although she had refused to dance with him, from dancing with anybody else. In conversation he was (6) "awkward and solemn, apologizing instead of attending."

'In his actual proposal Mr Collins (7) began with a conventional compliment, (8) continued with a speech subdivided into numbered paragraphs, (9) referred reverently to a titled patroness, (10) indulged the flattering hope that the patroness would approve of his choice, (11) mentioned four per cent in a financial passage, (12) stated that Elizabeth's refusal of him was one of the elegant manoeuvres which are customary, (13) never said he loved her.

'The heroines of Jane Austen, although the manners of her age were weighted against them, were coolly adept in disposing of unwelcome males. Men of letters have shown a taste for blunter, less refined methods of getting rid of the woman.

'In olden days men had two tremendous historical factors to help them in this aim. . . .'

At this point there was a buzz of interest from the audience, which had grown to 18. But it quickly subsided as the lecture continued: and Gattling ostentatiously put his feet up when Cogg continued:

'I mean, of course, Transport and Mythology. And by transport I mean slow transport. . . . For a Londoner, now, an important meeting in Birmingham or even New York, can be contained within 24 hours. But when the journey to Birmingham took the better part of three days, then the whole expedition might as well last a fortnight. In those days a journey of twenty miles needed more care and planning than we now take over a business trip to Antwerp. It was a cue for a farewell embrace. If James Boswell wanted to leave his wife in Edinburgh for four months, he only had to find it necessary to keep an appointment in London. Good for Boswell.'

At this point Cogg made the mistake of trying, and

failing, to wink: whereupon Gattling-Fenn interrupted with a 'Better still, possibly, for Mrs Boswell?'

Cogg was no good at impromptu answers to questions, so he pretended to take no notice.

'In Ancient Times,' he went on, 'the world's slow speed record, coupled with maximum separation from wife, was actually held by Odysseus, whose absence from Penelope was moreover chiefly concerned with the rescue of Helen (on the re-bound, it is pertinent to add, from the unsuccessful wooing of whom he had proposed to Penelope). The Odyssey was the world record retarded journey back (10 years to sail 296 miles).

'Yet even these time intervals are surpassed by the technique of the Mediaeval Tradition of Courtly Love.'

'L'amour courtoise?' said little G. Wert, the only person in the class who could speak French.

'If you like,' Cogg ad-libbed, not understanding. 'Courtly love,' he went on, 'has much to do with absences on journeys to win fame for the Lady's approval. The knight set himself Impossible Task services, rather in the mythology manner. Chaucer emphasizes the courtly love aspect of the Palaman and Arcite story in his version of it, the *Knight's Tale*. After the journeys, imprisonments, dismissals, releases, secret returns and disguises, the fights and tournaments which have to unfold themselves in courtly order between Palaman's love-at-first-sight glimpse of Emilia and his eventual marriage to her, something like 26 years passed. Parents who dislike long engagements should re-check by troubadour standards.'

At this point Odoreida started a slow handclap: but it was quickly shushed.

'Emilia may not have been aware of the cruder facts of courtly love life: The Famous Ulrick von Lichtenstein of history was the champion faithful knight of the thirteenth century, and on one devotional journey made in honour of his princess, he broke lances for her so successfully in his armed equestrian combat that the broken lance score, according to him, was 307: nil. All the more extraordinary is it, then, to learn that in the very midst of

The Von Lichtenstein collection of broken lances.

heroism for the Lady whom he had never touched, he
would from time to time take three days off to visit his
wife and children.

'In still earlier times the man seeking to lose the woman
could make use of an even more powerful weapon: namely "It is written". "It is the will of the gods".

'This was the method of Aeneas with Dido, Queen of
Carthage. Aeneas was able to combine ancient prophecies
with admonition from the ghost of his father.

'The leaving of Dido was not abandonment at its tough-
est. Aeneas was eight years late on his pre-ordained journey
to Latium already. But Dido gave Aeneas her hospitality
and her bed: she had had to listen to the Troy story for
the hundredth time. Moreover, Aeneas tried to sneak away.
But the trick was discovered. Now it had to be the "will
of the gods" or nothing. "I would stay", Aeneas said, "if
Fate would let me.

But now Grynaean prophecies
On Latium bid me fix my eyes."

Aeneas then had the good plan of invoking the ghost of
his father, if you will forgive my own rough translation,

Cogg continued, meaning that he was using the same crib:

> ' "My sire, Anchises, oft as night
> Invests the world, and stars are bright,
> Warns me in sleep with wrathful frown,
> And scares me on my couch of down. . . ."

In the end, Grynaean prophecies proved adequate. Aeneas certainly lost no face over this affair. On the contrary it intensified the atmosphere of the esteem, often a thought difficult to account for, by which his name is surrounded.

'Aeneas was an intellectual, and if he had lived a few thousand years later he would have played the part of the poet or artist, who, when he is tired of a woman, makes a great public point of doing nothing underhand or mean about it. He discusses it openly with the loved one he is about to wrong, explains that "wrong" is not the right word, states the whole situation with clinical objectivity, asks her about it, even expects her sympathy for his predicament, and does in fact occasionally, if not usually, borrow money from her in order to carry out his plan in style. He will point out that their union is no longer a "real" one, that as a marriage it is a marriage in name only and therefore not marriage at all, that She will be suffering a long decay of the spirit if She continues to stay with him, and much of this will be said so eloquently, so quite definitely for posterity, that it may blind the girl, and even posterity, to the fact that the real motive is, still, another woman.

'Shelley personifies this characteristic. He was a born proselytiser—of his close friends, of distant sympathizers, of his sisters when they were still schoolgirls, of their pretty little friend Harriet Westrook. Shelley fell in love with Harriet. *Let death all mortal ties dissolve,* he said. *But ours shall not be mortal.* Not mortal, that is, until Shelley wanted to leave Harriet for Mary Godwin.'

'Ditched her, I suppose?' said Odoreida, with a wheezy laugh. Cogg, who was reading his lecture from notes, and was incapable of answering back in any circumstances, pretended not to hear, and went on:

'Shelley was so splendidly above the battle, so delicately strong, so liberal, that he made the situation symbolic. He couldn't help enlarging on it, even to Harriet. He wrote her a letter:

' "Exhausted as I am with our interview I cannot refrain from writing to you. . . . Do remember that my feelings for you are unaltered. . . . I repeat (and believe me, for I am sincere) that my attachment to you is unimpaired. Our connection was not one of passion and impulse."

'Shelley says in effect, "I am leaving you for the sake of our souls." He did not say "I am leaving you for the sake of my work," though this was to become, soon, an approved method of self-extrication, very nineteenth century, very "genius is a law to itself."

"Genius—artist—artist in life. The man of talent must make use of the assumption that the man of genius makes his own code."Your career," they must surely say. Adolphe, in Benjamin Constant's novel, agrees warmly with "the truth" of his friend's suggestion: "She is ten years older than you . . . you will look after her for another 20 years . . . she will then be old . . . every road is open to you, but you must remember that, between you and all forms of success, there is one insurmountable obstacle—and that obstacle is Ellenore".

'The painter can look at the girl with screwed up eyes, head slightly on one side. It is an easy first step. For the moment, she is part of a picture, merely. It is a way of beginning to put the girl in the background. The author, when the woman seems to begin to lean a little heavily, may disengage his arm to make a note in the theatre programme or the restaurant menu. It is an accredited way of semi dismissal, a slight push on the shoulder. "That notebook. I knew you had that notebook" says the girl in Norman Mailer's short story. "Why, you're nothing but a notebook".'

I started a murmur of approval here. Cogg had managed to get in an O.K. modern author.

'The axiom that genius is a law to itself can be used as an emergency exit by men who have kept a small talent on the boil for so long that there is nothing left but vapour. More interesting are the real giants who have felt that genius, or a genius for personal freedom, is their justification.

' "You do not appreciate my genius," says Tolstoy in effect when as a young man he is breaking with Valeria. "You are angry because I am 'only able to deliver lectures' . . . These are all ideas and feelings which are very dear to me, which I write about almost with tears in my eyes".'

'In short, we must part.'

' "For the sake of my work." But there is one danger, one vital mistake, which must be avoided. Here, if anywhere, the questionable rule "never explain, never justify" must be applied. Gauguin is the myth personification of the artist who left his family for the sake of his genius. His action in the name of Art was unimpeachable. Yet his behaviour in the realm of human relationship was less than perfect. He could not "act in simplicity", he could not make his actions definite, he left broken edges, he wrote long letters of self-justification, he was always complaining that his children did not write to him. He even illustrated the strong tendency of the "offender" to take a strong moral tone about the rights of his behaviour.

'Now in the realm of Anti-Woo. . . .'

This was the last paragraph of Cogg-Willoughby's lecture. He had meant to say more, but Mr and Mrs Trensham had left the room, and Frith-Morteroy and Miss Feeling were talking in an undertone. Cogg had been on his feet for forty minutes; I thought it was time I stood up: so I rose, clapping my hands slowly and soundlessly together as if applauding and said:

'Mr Willoughby is prepared to answer any questions.'

Cogg sat down suddenly, and looked annoyed. There was a pause, which I quickly filled.

'What about Byron?' I said.

'Yes—rather,' said Cogg, diving into his notes again. 'I was going to say. . . .' He started reading again—not what I had intended, of course.

'The case of Byron is difficult, because although his dismissals were the most violent and the most brutal, the women seemed to like it—'

'I know,' Gattling said with a complacent grin. 'Be tough and they come swarming.'

Poor Gattling. To be successfully Byronic one must be perpetually pale. Gattling was rather the opposite. Cogg continued:

'When Byron deserted Lady Caroline Lamb, there was no word of apology. Instead he accused her of 'levities, caprices and mean subterfuges.' This had the effect of doubling the adoration of all his admirers. Byron redoubled by leaving England under a cloud. This master tactic I propose to call Brand of Cainism. Its characteristics are easy to analyze—.'

But not if you've lost a page of your Manuscript, which is what Cogg had done. Unwilling to watch Cogg fumble, I called the meeting to a close. Mrs Hopkins had cut some ham sandwiches for us the day before, and we regaled ourselves with champo, the new beverage. No formal vote of thanks was called for: yet Cogg had certainly set us talking.

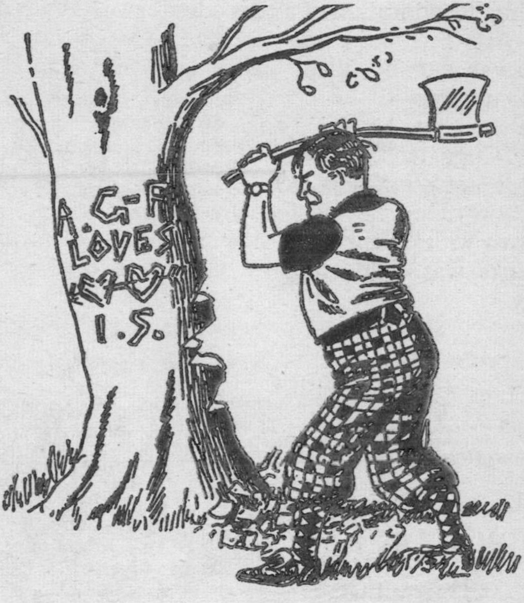
A. G-A
LOVER
I. S.

Index

A

'Asra,' poise of, counterployed, 83

Asterisks, use of, in sex literature, 15

Athlete's Foot, failure to conceal treatment of, 35

Authoress, female, as natural enemy of male author, 71-2

Avoidance gambits, 66ff

B

Bach, J. S. *Italian Concerto* of, hummed, 61

'Beaulieu', ex-perfect profile of, 28-9

Beauty, female, proved to exist, 25; 'attracts', 25; medical estimate of, 25; small talk recommended in association with, 26; self-protection ploys recommended when in ambience of, 25-9; traditional one-upness of, 75; bold counterploys aimed against, 76ff

Beethoven, Ludwig van, mentioned by Winkle, 38

Black Book of Unrecommended Retorts, 45

'Bloom' (Vera Bloomington), occasional necessity of getting rid of, 70

'Bouncing', dangers of, 32-3, 86

Brand of Cainism, 120

Browning, Robert, as subject of sonnet sequence, 71-2

Busardi, Dr, 46ff

C

Cigarette, provocative refusal of, 20

'Clare' (Clara Evelyn Blostock), basic gambit of, 33-4

Coad-Sanderson, G., attitude to pornography of, 16; his scale of Progressive Rifts, 85ff; life-long annoyance over costs of entertaining pretty theatre-lover, 105; technique of accusation, when in wrong, 104

Cogg-Willoughby, Howard, basic warm heartedness of, 97; his lecture on the Principles of Anti-Woo, 111-20

Compatibility, dangers of, 107

Concise Lifemanship Dictionary, The, 32

Cuffey, P. L. K., invisibility of, 53; bold attempt on girl, 53; ineffective taxi technique of, 54-5; failure with Mrs Gell, 55-6; with Madame Elsa, 56

More Humor in SIGNET Books

Light Fiction in SIGNET Editions

HOW RIGHT YOU ARE, JEEVES   by P. G. Wodehouse

With Jeeves, the prince of butlers, off on vacation, his bumbling master, Bertie Wooster, is left to struggle along as best he can, and the results are hilarious.

(#D2842—50¢)

BREAKFAST AT TIFFANY'S   by Truman Capote

The best-selling novel, also a Paramount film starring Audrey Hepburn as a whimsical young heroine; plus three superior short stories.   (#P2912—60¢)

HOW TO STEAL A MILLION   by Michael Sinclair

The wacky story of a lovely Parisian girl from a long line of art forgers, who makes her entry into the life of crime as a most uncommon thief. A movie starring Audrey Hepburn and Peter O'Toole.   (#P2958—60¢)

FAMOUS SHORT-SHORT STORIES

Short-short stories originally published in *Liberty* Magazine, by such outstanding authors as MacKinlay Kantor, Philip Wylie, Budd Shulberg, and John D. MacDonald.

(#P2896—60¢)

THE PERFECT MURDER   by H. R. F. Keating

Winner of the Crime Writers Association award for the best novel of 1964, *The Perfect Murder* has been hailed as one of the most original, imaginative, and wildly funny mysteries ever written.   (#P2884—60¢)

MORE ROMAN TALES   by Albert Moravia

Thirty-one vignettes of Roman life and character, narrated by the durable men and women of the Italian working classes. By Italy's foremost novelist.   (#P2671—60¢)

SHORT FRIDAY and Other Stories by Isaac Bashevis Singer

Remarkable tales, translated from the Yiddish, in which demons, witches, and angels turn up in everyday life, whether it is lived in a Polish village or in Brooklyn.

(#T2770—75¢)